Vittorio Di Martino is a native of Rome who lived and worked
in Ireland for ten years before moving to France to work in Switzerland.
While ancient Rome has been the focus of his classical studies,
his time in Ireland and Switzerland provided an opportunity
to study the Celtic world and its contacts with the
Mediterranean world.

ROMAN IRELAND

VITTORIO DI MARTINO

The Collins Press

Published in 2003 by
The Collins Press,
West Link Park,
Doughcloyne,
Wilton,
Cork

Copyright © Vittorio Di Martino

Vittorio Di Martino has asserted his right to be identified as author of this work.

British Library Cataloguing in Publication data.

Di Martino, Vittorio
Roman Ireland
1. Romans – Ireland 2. Latin language – influence on Irish
3. Ireland – Civilisation – Roman influences 4. Ireland –
History – to 1172
I. Title
936.1'04
ISBN 1903464196

Printed in Ireland by Colour Books

This book is printed on uncoated paper manufactured with the greatest possible care for the environment.

Typesetting by The Collins Press

Typeface Sabon 11 point

Cover photograph: fragment of a fourth-century AD Roman silver serving dish
from the Balline hoard, courtesy National Museum of Ireland

Author's comments on indented quotations in square brackets

Contents

To Roswitha, my love and wife,
and our daughters, Kirsten and Astrid

LIST OF ILLUSTRATIONS

MAPS

PREFACE

Imagining Ireland as an untouched 'virgin', immune from Roman influence during the four centuries that Britain, only thirty miles away at the closest crossing, was a centre of *Romanitas*, has always struck me as an absurdity, comparable to imagining an island thirty miles away from New York still being inhabited by incommunicado Iroquois Indians. Communications were different, of course, in the two periods but thirty miles were nothing even in Roman times for sailors who routinely navigated from one side to another of the entire Mediterranean Sea, not by chance called *Mare nostrum*.

However, until recently, the official position was that there was no Roman expedition to Ireland, with little trade or cultural influence. Only after the fall of the Roman empire did St Patrick come bringing with him Christianity and opening a new Celtic era which was the basis for national culture and identity.

In recent times, while fully recognising the uniqueness of the Irish culture, a more considered approach has been emerging which emphasises the importance of the influence exerted by the Roman civilisation on Ireland. It is now authoritatively recognised that Ireland did not escape Roman influence. Roman objects, for example were introduced to Ireland in much greater numbers than had been believed and the total sum of Roman influence in Ireland was, in any event, greater than that represented by such objects.

The key role of Rome's contribution to the shaping of Irish art has been progressively understood, as has the early influence exerted by the Latin language in pre-Patrician Ireland and the crucial function of trade in opening new routes from the Roman to the Irish world. Even the influence of Roman technology and farming methods on Irish dairying and cultivation is being progressively disclosed. Finally, the entire issue of a Roman invasion is the object of a very lively debate.

The aim of this book is to contribute to, and further enhance, the ongoing debate in this area with four main targets in mind:

– to produce an independent and balanced history of the interrelationship between Rome and Ireland in classical and post-classical times, looking in a positive way to the enrichment of cultures rather than emphasising parochial boundaries;

– to achieve an overall understanding of cultural influences beyond sectorial specialisations and disciplines' fragmentation, by dealing with all relevant areas of work in an integrated way;

– to extend considerably the period of time usually covered by other works treating this topic. There is in fact no reason to limit the period under investigation to the period of the Roman presence in Britain. Roman influence in Ireland started much earlier than AD 43 and terminated at a much later date than the beginning of the fifth century. Roman and sub-Roman culture substantially influenced Ireland up to the arrival of Vikings in AD 800;

— to avoid analysing Irish history in isolation, as is often the case, this book looks at Irish events and culture in a broader historical context, taking full account of major developments in Roman and Celtic culture elsewhere which have a direct or indirect bearing on Ireland.

The aim is very ambitious and one that would scare most experts in this area. Furthermore the area in itself is a minefield loaded with ideological controversies, vested interests and personal pride. It comes as no surprise that nobody has yet embarked on a work like this. Being an outsider and an amateur, I have the advantage of feeling absolutely free to express my opinions and views on the subject. By deeply loving my town of origin – Rome – and the country where I spent many years of my adult life – Ireland – I am in the fortunate position to make only mistakes to the best of my understanding and good faith. I also know my limits. But exploring this 'forgotten' area was something that had to be done and I have taken my courage in both hands and done it. *What is done cannot be undone.*

Acknowledgements

Numerous experts and organisations have provided me with advice, guidance and information in the preparation of this work. Some are cited in the text and in the references to each chapter but I wish to thank them all for their most valuable contribution to the making of this book.

Grateful thanks are also due for permission to reproduce the following maps and figures by publishers, institutions and individuals: map 3 and figures 2, 3, 4, 10, 12, 13 by permission Royal Irish Academy; map 4 by permission A&C Publishers and Emania; figure 1 by permission L. Laing; map 5 by permission of the controller of HMSO; figures 5 and 6 by permission Society of Antiquaries of London; map 6 by permission Cork Historical and Archaeological Society; figure 7 and map 9 by permission Emania; figure 8 by permission D.J. Breeze; figure 9 by permission University of Wales Press; figure 11 by permission E. Bourke; map 8 by permission S. Johnson; figure 14 by permission A. Brindley; figure 15 by permission Stationery Office Dublin; figure 16 by permission Emania and National Museum of Ireland; figure 17 by permission the controller of HMSO and M.J. Green; figure 18 by permission Bompiani Publisher and Pontificum Collegium Germanicum and Hungaricum in Rome; figure 18 by permission J. Cunningham; figure 21 by permission British Museum Press, Pindar Press and Trinity College Library Dublin; figure 22 by permission Speculum; figure 23 by permission British Museum.

Finally I must express my gratitude to Jenny and Helen Sabine; Ursula O'Donovan for editing; and to Daniele Hugon for the electronic drafting of maps 1, 2 and 7.

VITTORIO DI MARTINO
DECEMBER 2002

CHAPTER 1

The First Invasion

In my view the answer is overwhelmingly 'yes' – the Romans did invade Ireland.
R. Warner

There is, as yet, no archaeological evidence for a Roman invasion of Ireland.
J.D. Bateson

THE MAIN AREA OF CONTROVERSY
The general was a living legend. Since he had become the governor of Britain in AD 77, Gnaeus Julius Agricola had annihilated the Ordovices, definitely conquered the Druidic stronghold in the island of Anglesey and had secured the Roman presence in Wales. Moving to the north, he had subjugated the Votadini and the Selgovae, brought his troops to the fringe of the Scottish highlands and had defeated the assembled tribes of Caledonia in the battle of Mons Graupius. By AD 84 he had extended Roman rule as far as it ever had been in Britain.

Agricola's life, in fortune and misfortune, had criss-crossed the histories of three of the greatest emperors in Rome: Vespasianus (AD 69-79); Titus (AD 79-81) and Domitianus (AD 81-96).

Only nineteen in AD 59, he had served as a military tribune in Britain on the staff of the governor Suetonius Paulinus. There he had met the young Titus and formed a friendship which, when Titus' father,

Vespasian, became emperor, gained him rapid promotion to legionary commander and, eventually, the governorship of Britain.

The principate of Titus which followed, was marked by a policy of maximum expansion in the region. This was the opportunity Agricola had long been waiting for, the chance to make his more audacious dreams become reality. The period was, however, too short to exploit the advantages of such a policy in full. Soon things started to change. When Titus' younger brother Domitianus rushed to Rome (Titus was dying) to be acclaimed emperor by the troops and the Senate, Agricola knew his prime had passed.

Since he had been denied the title of *participes imperii* (the sharing of imperial responsibilities) with Titus, Domitianus had been resentful towards his brother and his entourage. Now he had a free hand, but he hesitated for some time before recalling Agricola to Rome.

At first, he confirmed him in his governorship, hoping to gain much needed glory from the general's continuing victories. Progressively, however, imperial attention shifted elsewhere with a difficult war in Germany against the Chatti and the opening of a new front in Dacia. Britain was not a priority any more. When eventually Domitianus decided to call the general back, in AD 84, this was done with all honours, but the people of Rome cried shame and the emperor was accused of being jealous of such a valiant man. Agricola was offered the proconsulship of Asia, which he refused. When he died in AD 93, the public rumour was that he had been poisoned by order of Domitianus.

While a legend in life, the general was given everlasting fame in his biography *Agricola* by Publius Cornelius Tacitus, perhaps the greatest of all Roman historians. Their lives, too, had crossed. In AD 77, the year Agricola had been named governor of Britain, Tacitus had married his daughter.

The information given in *Agricola* is first-hand, exemplary in accuracy and detail, straight to the point and written in a style characterised by literary rigour. After 2,000 years we still call a work with those rare qualities *tacitean*. Altogether, Tacitus is simply the best source for the history of Britain in that period.

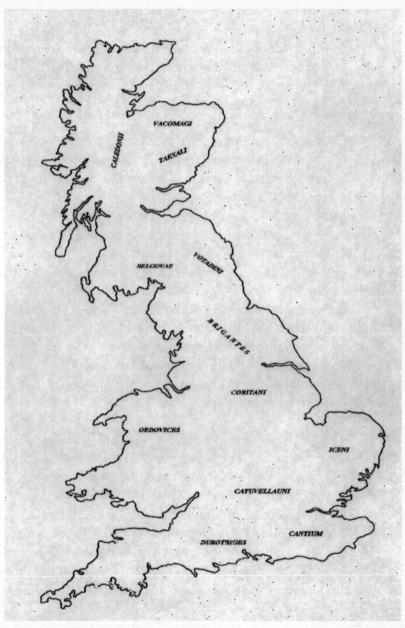

Map 1. The tribes of Britain in Roman times.

There is no subsequent period in the history of Roman Britain, or even in the early history of Anglo-Saxon England, for which we have a similarly detailed narrative from a written source. Indeed, if we wished to find a parallel, we should need to look as far forward as the ninth century to the account given in the Anglo-Saxon Chronicle of the movements of the great Danish army which landed in East Anglia in 865.[1]

Despite general recognition of the importance of the source, there is a passage in *Agricola* which has given rise to a most controversial debate. Tacitus refers to having heard his father-in-law several times affirming that Ireland could be conquered with one legion and a few auxiliaries.[2] This statement, to use a euphemism, was never very popular in Ireland: 'The Irish writers, jealous of their national honour, are extremely provoked on this occasion, both with Tacitus and with Agricola', says E. Gibbon, author of the classical *The History of the Decline and Fall of the Roman Empire.*[3]

Indeed, no other statement could have touched more on the main strongholds of Irish identity. On the one hand, the 'uniqueness' of Irish civilisation, unconquered until the peaceful invasion of St Patrick and Christianity. On the other, the bravery of the Celtic warriors, and the myth of individual excellence in war, to be defeated only by the number, not the quality of enemy troops.

The really vast chasm of difference between the cultures of Britain and Ireland and the rest of Europe was that the Four Green Fields of this island were never occupied or raided or touched by the Roman Empire. No Roman centurion set foot on Irish soil, and the Legions and the conquering eagle were never seen on the Irish shore. Ireland was just that too much farther away to interest the hairy little men from Italy, who had conquered the whole of the known world and its barbaric hordes by their skill in arms, their discipline, their law and order and their straight roads, and Roman towns, and baths, and fortress camps. All Gaul and Britain had been subdued by the military superiority of the Roman army and its mercenaries and its accompanying culture. Ireland missed all this. No Roman roads, no iron discipline, no mercenary troops to fight alongside the Legions. The result was Ireland remained Celtic.[4]

Although this traditional approach is questioned by new evidence and progressively abandoned by the better scholars, when it comes to the possibility of an invasion even the more open-minded appear reluctant to tackle the subject directly. Few dare to enter the field and those who do appear hesitant and almost apologetic. The word invasion is handled with caution and intrusion is often used as a substitute.

Beyond this reticence, a series of questions still require an answer. Are the sources reliable? Was the invasion feasible and if so, what was its rationale? If an invasion took place, who was involved and when? From where was it launched and where did the troops land? Are there traces left in Ireland and, most importantly, did it really take place?

THE QUALITY OF THE SOURCES

Tacitus is the primary source. No other can be compared to him in importance and reliability. Furthermore, in this case, Tacitus tells us about information personally gathered from Agricola. The only potential drawback lies in the possibility that Tacitus, influenced by family ties, has provided us with an overly-laudatory version of events or was himself fed with exaggerated accounts by Agricola.

Would this make Agricola a liar and Tacitus an encomiast ready to distort the truth? Either way is difficult to believe.

The life of the general leaves little doubt about his honesty and integrity. Moreover, it could be argued that an intended or even actual invasion of Ireland, seen from the Roman side, would not have added much to the reputation of Agricola, especially if it was abortive. Why jeopardise such a reputation with a false statement?

Similar considerations are equally valid for Tacitus. Tacitus was not immune from encomiastic writing and he is not immune from it in *Agricola* either. He can omit information but he does not manipulate facts. The quality of his information is far superior to that of all previous writers about Ireland. No more cannibalism and incestuous habits.[5] With

Tacitus, for the first time, Ireland stops being fantasyland and becomes a real country similar in many respects to nearby Britain. It should also be noted that *Agricola* was written in AD 98, only five years after the death of the general when the memory of Agricola was still fresh in the minds of many people who had been his contemporary. Tacitus would have had no reason and no opportunity to distort the facts.

If Tacitus is reliable, as he appears to be, other parts of *Agricola* become immediately relevant in support of a possible Roman invasion of Ireland. Tacitus tells us that in his fifth campaign, in AD 82, Agricola brought under his control tribes previously 'unknown' and that he fortified that part of Britain which looks towards Ireland. Later in the text, he mentions that traders were familiar with Ireland's ports and harbours and that Agricola was on friendly terms with an exiled king from that country, hoping to make use of him should the occasion arise. These are essential parts of the story and will be dealt with in greater detail later.

Another Roman source makes reference to a Roman invasion of Ireland. The poet Juvenal mentions in his *Satirae* that 'Roman arms have been carried beyond the shores of Ireland'.

Since Juvenal is not an historian, his statement has consequently been ignored or dismissed as a rhetorical flourish. However, it was possibly written no more than ten years after Agricola's death, when, as for Tacitus' *Agricola,* memories were too fresh to allow a manipulation of facts. It deserves more attention.

Juvenal was not keen on hyperbolical statements and exaggerated conclusions. He was a tragic figure and a combatant with a profound sense of justice and an abhorrence of falsehood and abuse.

He had studied rhetoric and extensively used it in his works. Apparently he had practised declamation in Rome for a large part of his life: in his seventh epigram, Martial regards Juvenal as *facundus* (eloquent). Rhetoric was an essential part of the formative background of the cultivated citizen and was held in high regard in Rome. Juvenal's rhetoric belongs to this tradition:

In general, his frequent historical references are not only rhetorically effective,

6

but also accurate and capable of ample certification. Much of his best work in the ten satires in particular depends for its effect upon historical truth; the implication that his 'rhetoric' is careless in this respect is quite unfair. His moral elevation and fierce indignation against current abuses presuppose a regard for truth; and the questioning and the incredulous temper that he often displays, especially with regard to Greek legends and history, implies a claim to historic insight and accuracy on his own part.[6]

In particular, the credibility of Juvenal's statement on Ireland is reinforced by the reference, in the second part of the sentence, to the Romans having 'taken' the Orkney islands, which is historically true. It has also been suggested that Juvenal had served in the army in Britain under Agricola. An inscription found at Aquinum, his native town, records the dedication of an offering to Ceres by Iunium Juvenalis belonging to a cohort of Dalmatians.

Dalmatian cohorts served all around the empire and cohorts I, II and IV operated in Britain at the end of the first century. Juvenal was born *c.* AD 60, so he would have been the correct age. Some biographies of Juvenal refer to the military appointment of the poet in the British isles, though most biographies place Juvenal's appointment in Egypt, where he was exiled by Domitian at the end of his life.

There is, however, a most intriguing find in Ireland that seems to provide evidence in support of Juvenal's words. In 1934, the Cardiff trawler 'Muroto' was fishing on the Porcupine bank, 150 miles off the west coast of Ireland, 150 fathoms of water (approximately 275 metres), when it dredged up a storage jar, an *olla*. The shape of the vessel and the quality of the ware show a Romano-British origin. In the absence of the rim and shoulders, it is difficult to fix the date of the vessel but, judging by its general character, it is not likely to be later than the second century AD.[7]

Why was a Roman *olla* being carried and by whom in such distant waters? We do not know. But we know that the timing is consistent with the Juvenal and Tacitus narratives, and Juvenal's statement that Roman arms had been carried *beyond* the shores of Ireland is certainly reinforced by this find.

Other Roman sources are late and not reliable. As to Irish sources, they simply do not exist. In the first century AD Ireland was still an illiterate country. Even this has been used as an argument against the possibility of an invasion. If the invasion took place only a few centuries before the beginning of literacy in Ireland, it would, the argument runs, be most unlikely that later versions of local sagas and legends did not report an event of such importance. This relies on the assumption that sagas and legends somehow mirror real past events.

It is not necessarily the case. Already at the beginning of this century the great French historian Camille Julian was highlighting the problem in his monumental *Histoire de la Gaulle*:

These documents in the British language, mythological Irish cycles, etc, are often artificial works due to the imagination or erudition of storytellers and demi-sages. They are far from being a faithful representation of Ireland and do not necessarily reflect its beliefs and traditions. Too much personal imagination is hidden there, too many alterations have taken place.[8]

In the last twenty years these concepts have been strongly reiterated by the new Irish school of historical rationalism, arguing that most legends have no relationship with the past and are, instead, medieval fabrication. Even when some historical value is acknowledged to old sagas and legends, a proper distinction should be maintained between the reporting of facts in sagas and legends that presumably happened centuries before, and contemporary, historical Roman sources.

WAS AN INVASION FEASIBLE?
According to Tacitus, Agricola's answer to this question was yes, with as small a force as a legion and some auxiliaries. Was this a gross miscalculation by the general? It is possible but not probable.

The qualities of Agricola as a general have already been described. But Agricola also had, perhaps more than anyone else at that time, a complete understanding of the military scene in the region. In his youth he had participated as a military tribune under the command of

Suetonius Paulinus in two of the most momentous and bloody episodes of the conquest of Britain: the attack on Anglesey and the repression of Queen Boudicca's revolt in AD 60-61. The final battle, somewhere in the midlands, saw, according to Dio Cassius, about 10,000 men from the fourteenth and the twentieth legions, as well as auxiliary troops, facing and defeating an enormous force, perhaps as many as 230,000 men, on Boudicca's side. This data, certainly a gross exaggeration, gives, however, a clear idea of the extreme disproportion in numbers between Roman and local troops, actually occurring in this kind of war.

Ten years later Agricola was again in Britain and in command of the twentieth legion. From AD 71-AD73 he participated, under the governorship of Petilius Cerialis, in the conquest of the Brigantes and the occupation of new territories at least as far north as Carlisle. It was not an easy job. According to Tacitus it involved 'many battles, some not unbloody'.

Thus, by the time he became governor, Agricola was already an accomplished general. He had gained enormous field experience, including mountain warfare and seaborne operations. Most of all, he knew well how to deal with the most bellicose tribes of the region.

This was the kind of man that, as reported in 'Agricola', had affirmed Ireland could be conquered with one legion and few auxiliary troops. A legion was the backbone of the imperial army, consisting of more than 5,000 men, still all Roman citizens at the time of Agricola, fully equipped and trained – one of the most powerful war machines of all times. A legion was a rare combination of cohesion and autonomy. Within the legion there were ten cohorts and within each cohort six centuries of 80 men. Supplementing the legions were selected troops from all around the empire, the auxiliaries. At the time of Agricola auxiliary units included the *cohors peditata,* composed of six centuries of infantry with 80 men each, the *cohort equitata,* a mix of cavalry and infantry, and the most prestigious of all, the *ala.* Within each *ala*, there were sixteen *turmae* of cavalry with 32 men each.

On the opposite side, the Celts were some of the most terrible warriors in ancient times. The historian Polybius has left us one of the best accounts of Celtic troops in battle, when describing the battle of

Talamon in 225 BC.

> On the other hand the fine order and the noise of the Celtic host horrified the Romans; for there were countless trumpets and horn blowers and since the whole army was shouting its war cries at the same time there was such a confused sound that the noise seemed to come not only from the trumpeters and the soldiers but also from the countryside which was joining in the echo. No less terrifying were the appearance and gestures of the naked warriors in front, all of whom were in the prime of life and of excellent physique. All the warriors in the front ranks were adorned with gold torcs and armlets. The Romans were particularly terrified by the sight of these men ...[9]

However, by the time of Agricola, Romans knew the weak points of the Celtic troops and how to combat them efficiently. The equipment of the Celtic warrior was inferior to that of the Roman soldier. In most cases their shields were their only armour and were not sufficient to cover their whole body, usually naked in battle. Another disadvantage was that the Celts' shields were of wood so that they could be pierced or have spears stuck into them in so great a number as to make the shield too heavy to carry. The Celtic swords were longer than the Roman ones, good for cutting but not for thrusting and were more suitable for individual duels than for close combat between troops.

Romans also knew that Celtic courage and boldness were only one side of the coin. The other side was represented by a lack of determination when things were turning for the worst. There was also little cohesion among the different tribes participating in battle, and extreme individualism. According to Polybius, the Celts were incapable of forward planning or consistent practice.

Substantial intelligence was available to Agricola. Trade with Ireland had long been established and merchants were likely to provide him with the information needed about the island. As Agricola says: 'The interior parts are little known, but through commercial intercourse and the merchants there is better knowledge of the harbours and approaches.'[10]

In addition, several tribes in Ireland had some kind of connection with Britain: the Briganti were in both countries and the Irish Menapii were 'parallelled' by a Cohors I Menapiorum in the Roman army in Britain. They could all provide information and contacts for possible alliances on the occasion of a future campaign.

In light of these considerations, Agricola's appreciation as to the number of men needed for an invasion of Ireland becomes more realistic. Britain had been conquered with four legions and three were on duty at the time of Agricola. Since Ireland was one-third the size of Britain (as was known to Agricola), one legion would be sufficient, especially if supplemented by auxiliary troops and if the purpose of the first attack was a temporary invasion, rather than a long term territorial conquest similar to Caesar's first expedition to Britain in 55 BC, which had been carried out, perilously, with only two legions. However, it must be said, Agricola did not match the military genius of Caesar.

THE RATIONALE FOR AN INVASION

The personal position and interest of Caesar and Agricola may have played an important role in triggering decisions on the opportunity of an invasion.

In the case of Caesar, there was the need to maintain a high profile in front of the Roman public in a year which was not offering much to him on the political scene. Pompey and Crassus were the two consuls in Rome designated for AD 55. Keeping to the agreement he himself had with the other two *triumviri* meant Caesar had to find alternatives for action in that year. Britain was his opportunity. There was also the risk of being recalled to Rome, losing both the command of his troops and the immunities he was enjoying due to his status.

Similarly, for Agricola, after four years of campaigning, the pacification of Wales and the building up of a fortified *limes* in the north between the Clyde and Forth, most of the objectives of his governorship seemed to have been achieved. 'If the valour of our armies and the glory of the Roman name should allow it, in Britain proper (*Britannia ipsa*) a limit of advance was found,' says Tacitus. In Britain maybe, but not as far as

Ireland was concerned. With Ireland as the new target, nobody would acknowledge the fact that Agricola's term of office was expiring and that he should be recalled. His immediate predecessors, Petillius Cerialis and Julius Frontinus, had been in charge for no more than four years each. Agricola managed to keep his governorship for at least six.

On a broader, regional perspective, Agricola was certainly interested, as Caesar had been when attacking Britain, in removing the bad example of populations belonging to the same Celtic culture enjoying their freedom from Rome in a totally independent territory. In both cases, the military situation was not completely under control. It was a high risk to engage in the adventure of a seaborne operation in perilous seas under unsettled conditions.

Caesar took the risk and paid the price. Due to the need to deal with a new uprising in Gaul and Germany in 55 BC, his expedition was launched very late in the season and suffered the initial disaster of a storm destroying most of his fleet. The Roman army, without cavalry and stores, seemed for a while at the mercy of the enemy. Only Caesar's determination and imagination managed to redress the situation.

Was Agricola ready to take similar risks? The situation was rather different in his case. Irish tribes were not fuelling a revolt and supplying tribes in Britain with help in their fight against the Romans, nor were they, at the time, rendering the sea insecure by acts of piracy. All good reasons to make the choice uncertain. The final decision would eventually depend on more important factors closely linked to the shaping of imperial policies in the capital of the Empire, more than 2,000 kilometres away.

Imperial policies regarding Britain had been undergoing varying phases in the previous decades. This was the only part of the empire where an active policy of conquest of new territories was seriously being pursued in the second half of the first century. It was a policy which required sustained effort and the engagement of important resources. It could not be undertaken and maintained on the basis of only local considerations. A much broader perspective was needed which would take into account the global interests of the empire. The almost 30 legions of Rome could not be used indifferently.

If an aggressive policy was undertaken in Britain, less ambitious policies had to be implemented in the other two unsettled regions of the empire: Germany and the Orient. The imperial policies in respect of already pacified regions also came into consideration since the status of such regions and of the populations could play an essential role in guaranteeing their loyalty to Rome in difficult situations. The concrete mix of such policies at a given time also depended upon such circumstances as the fight for power in Rome and the background and attitude of each emperor.

In AD 43 Claudius had made Britain a priority and had personally led the Roman army in the breaking of British resistance at *Camulodunum* (Colchester). Internally, he needed strong military recognition to reinforce his power and was ready to renounce an active policy in Germany in favour of the more visible intervention in Britain.

Ten years later, this policy was put at risk. The new emperor, Nero, even considered abandoning Britain. A new front had been opened in Armenia and the Roman army was involved in a difficult war which ended in AD 58, only to start again a few years later. This required a colossal effort in the region both in military and financial terms. In AD 63, the year in which the Armenian war eventually finished, Nero was forced into a heavy devaluation of the Roman currency. There was little room for an expansionist policy in Britain although Rome was obliged to deal with this region to counter an almost continuous series of rebellions which culminated in Boudicca's revolt of AD 60.

At the death of Nero in AD 68, imperial policies in Britain changed again. The new emperor, Vespasianus, was keen on promoting a more active role for the Roman army in that country. British legions, with the exception of the Legio II Augusta that he had once commanded while in Britain, had not shown great sympathy for his cause during the ferocious civil war which brought him to power. Another Legio II, recruited from marines of the Ravenna fleet during the civil war, had by contrast, greatly contributed to his victory. The presence of this legion in Britain would be an example. Before appointing it to its new duty, the Emperor rewarded the legion, originally composed of auxiliaries, with a permanent status and granted the additional titles of *pia fidelis* (pious and faithful) as a recognition of its fidelity. More action and new chiefs would certainly help in guaranteeing the fidelity of the other troops.

In AD 71, Vespasianus appointed the excellent Cerialis as the new governor of Britain, and Agricola was named commander of the twentieth legion which had been the most reluctant to join his cause. In the spring of the same year his son Titus was in Rome celebrating his victory in Giudea. The closing of this important front allowed for the redeployment of important resources. The door was open for what would prove to be the beginning of a succession of great commanders and excellent armies and for an expansionist policy in Britain.

It is in the context of this policy that the rationale for an invasion of Ireland by Agricola must be viewed. This was a most propitious moment and conditions were specially favourable. If an invasion took place, it is likely to have taken place in this period. But when exactly? Is it possible to give a more precise date?

DATING THE INVASION

Again it all depends upon Tacitus' *Agricola*. This time it is not a matter of believing or not what Tacitus says, but of interpreting correctly his words, or more precisely the following sentence in *Agricola:*

> In the fifth season of campaigning he crossed in the first ship, and in frequent successful engagements brought under his control tribes previously unknown. Also, he fortified that part of Britain which looks toward Ireland, not through fear but rather in hope.[11]

Exactly one century ago this sentence became the object of a momentous academic dispute between two of the leading authorities on this subject. The battlefield was the *Classical Review* and the dispute was protracted over several years with an intensity of tone, barely avoiding becoming personal on several occasions.

It all started with an article written by Professor A. Gudeman in Philadelphia under the innocuous title of 'Notes to the Agricola of Tacitus' which appeared in the October issue of the *Review* in 1897. A small footnote in the commentary to the above sentence was the cause of this endless controversy: 'The absurdity of this violent change [another reading of the original manuscript] will become the more manifest, when the conviction has gained ground, as I am confident it will, that the whole chapter is unintelligible except on the presumption of an expedition to Ireland.'[12]

The reaction was both quick and tough. In the same year, Professor F. Haverfield, an authority in Britain, published in the *Review* a short, dismissive reply to Gudeman's article. 'This theory seems to me wholly mistaken.' Also, most disgracefully, Gudeman had not taken into account Haverfield's own interpretation of Tacitus' text. 'Mr Gudeman does not think my explanation even worthy of rejection.'

Gudeman did not give up. The following year he fired back a paper which appeared in the *Proceedings of the American Philological Association*.[13] This time he organised his reasoning in favour of the invasion around nine points, arguing in detail on each one of them. This was more than a sufficient challenge for Haverfield. In an article again in the *Classical Review*, entitled 'Did Agricola Invade Ireland?', he proceeded with a systematic dismantling of his adversary's theory point by point. A short reply to this article by Haverfield in the same issue of the *Review* put an end, for the time being, to the dispute.

It did not, however, end Gudeman's conviction that Ireland had been invaded by Agricola. Almost 30 years later he restated his position in yet another edition of his 'Notes to Tacitus De Vita Julii Agricolae'. This time, however, he recognised the value of his former adversary. 'Finally, our archaeological knowledge of Britain, under the brilliant leadership of late Professor Haverfield ... was greatly increased and put upon a sound scientific basis.'[14]

This is the story of the dispute, but what in particular were Gudeman and Haverfield arguing about and why was it such an intense and long-lasting dispute? The reason lies in the fact that Tacitus gives a clear date for the events described in this part of *Agricola* and that such events are directly related to an invasion of Ireland. The question is: exactly how are they related? If interpreted as an 'intention' to invade, the date given by

Tacitus is of limited interest. If, on the other hand, the interpretation is for an 'actual' invasion, the invasion would have occurred in the fifth season of campaigning, in AD 82.

The points of dispute were related to the significance and interpretation of a number of words in the Latin text. In particular, the words *prima nave transgressus* (he crossed in the first ship) were read by Gudeman as referring to the crossing of the Irish Sea for the first time by a Roman fleet, instead of just a crossing of the Solway or the Clyde by Agricola on a recognisance. This led straight to the central point in the dispute. The interpretation of the phrase *ignotas ad id tempus gentes ... domuit* (brought under control tribes previously unknown). Could this phrase be referring to Irish tribes or was it simply referring to Caledonian ones?

Irish tribes were certainly unknown to the Romans, yet Caledonians had previously been contacted. They would, therefore, not have been referred to as 'unknown', unless there were other Caledonian tribes not yet contacted by the Romans, or that the tribes Tacitus refers to were elsewhere, ie, on the Isle of Man. Neither suggestion is very convincing. It seems unlikely that after two years of campaigning in Scotland there were still unknown Caledonian tribes, and there is no evidence to support the hypothesis of a Roman invasion of the Isle of Man.

What is certain is that the sentence concerning the conquest of tribes previously unknown is in Chapter 24 of the *Agricola,* which is devoted to Ireland. This is the first positive correlation which emerges when reading the text in a comprehensive manner. Other interpretations are possible but they need to be justified on their own and not just in terms of a rejection of that correlation. This has not been done up to now. The arguments in favour of an identification of the unknown tribes as Irish seem prevailing at this stage and consequently the dating of the first invasion of Ireland to AD 82.

Whilst AD 82 is a very likely date, it would be a mistake to make it the only date. Ireland was certainly not invaded before AD 82 and, if not in that year, there is a strong possibility that it was invaded in the years which followed since all the basic preconditions for an invasion had been established by then.

DEPARTURE AND LANDING SITES

Attacking from the North was the natural option. Agricola had been carrying out naval and land operations along the coasts of Scotland between the Solway Firth and the Firth of Clyde for several years and had strongly garrisoned the entire area.

> In the lands up to the Tyne-Solway line at least 40 forts were held, of which all but seven were on new foundations. In a lowland Scotland there were at least further twenty forts or fortlets, and north of the Forth another nine or ten in addition to the legionary fortress.[15]

Particularly along the shores and in the hinterland of the Solway, Roman presence was impressive. On the northern side of the Firth stood the forts of Gatehouse, of Fleet, Glenlochar and Birrens (*Blatobulgium*) with additional Roman presence at Ward Law and Annan. This first line was backed by the forts of Dalwinston in the Nith Valley and Broomholm on the East. On the southside the fortress of Carlisle (*Luguvanium*) was the main stronghold of a defensive-offensive system including the forts of *Maglonat* (Old Carlisle), Caermote and *Alauna* (Maryport).

Although of different size, Glenlochar, Birrens and Maryport were able to house, and certainly the last two did in the following years, the new *cohortis millaria* created during the reign of Vespasian when the organisation of the Roman army underwent important reforms. These new units included 1,000 men each at least. Dalwinston contained a large concentration of military works, all of Flavian date, including a 62-acre camp at Bankfoot. Broomholm and Carlisle also housed significant Roman forces. Altogether Agricola should have been able to raise the equivalent of one legion and the few auxiliaries he considered necessary for an attack on Ireland almost entirely from the Solway area.

In the year AD 82 he was ready to launch the attack. As Tacitus tells us, 'he moved his troops in that part of Britain which looks towards Ireland in hope [of an invasion], rather than in fear' [of an attack from that country]. According to Gudeman the invasion moved from

Uxellodunum (Stanwicks), passed the Isle of Man and landed somewhere south of Donaghadee, near Belfast Lough.

This is a classical landing. Edward Bruce landed there in 1315 and William III in 1609. Still today this is the landing place for the ferry boats from Liverpool, Preston, Heysham and Stanraer. There, in *c.* 1850, at a place named 'Loughey', whose exact location is still a mystery, a hoard of Roman objects of the first century AD was discovered in association with a burial place. Even if the burial place was destroyed by the finder interested only in the hoard, the association is crucial to the archaeological value of the findings.

Roman artefacts, particularly coins, have often been accused of being out of context and simply dismissed as late imports by collectors or antiquarians. The same problem exists, of course, for Irish objects, but it is certainly not emphasised in the same way. Not only are some of the greatest Irish metalworks, such as the Moylough belt shrine, the Tara brooch and the Ardagh chalice 'without association', but for many of them the place of provenance is not even known. For a number of objects, including some of the most famous illuminated manuscripts, their Irish origin is even a matter of debate. It is sufficient to look at the catalogue of one of the most important exhibitions of Celtic metalwork held in 1989 in the British Museum to realise that ten per cent of all the objects in that catalogue are either 'unprovenanced' or generally attributed to 'Ireland'.[16]

It is important to recognise that the problem of provenance is a general problem with Irish findings and cannot be used in a selective way for Roman findings only.

> [Irish] artefacts that can be attributed to the final centuries of the first millennium BC and the opening ones of the Christian era are more numerous and more diverse in type [than previous ones] ... Unfortunately, once again the vast majority are without provenance and just as unfortunate is the fact that in the past many fell at one stage or other into the hands of dealers and collectors who had little time for such a seemingly unimportant detail as exact provenance ...[17]

The case of burials, however, is a special one. The origin and context of the objects found there are usually beyond suspicion because of their close association with human remains. Roman burials in Ireland are few but, for this reason, extremely important. The 'Loughey' burial is one of them. Its contents consisted of several bronze tweezers, two bronze rings, a bronze fibula, the bowl of a spoon, 152 coloured glass beads, an armlet of purple glass, an armlet of Kimmeridge shale, a brass coin and other objects less well recorded.[18] Some of these objects have been lost. The others are now dispersed between the British Museum and the Ashmolean Museum in Oxford. But are they really Roman?

It has been argued that they suggest 'a background among the pre-Roman native people of southern Britain'[19], and on this basis rejected as Roman objects.[20] However, the solution is not so simple. In the report of this hoard which appeared six years after its discovery in the *Journal of the Royal Society of Antiquaries of Ireland*, it is indicated that the brass coin found in the hoard, now lost, was Roman and of the Upper Empire.[21] The links between objects found in Ireland and the Roman world are often subtle and complex and cannot be reduced to a simple yes/no alternative.

A typical example are the Irish 'La Tène' objects which are common Irish findings up to the arrival of Christianity. The 'La Tène' Celtic culture is named after a deposit of objects dating from the second century BC that were discovered in 1856 on the shores of Lake Neuchâtel in Switzerland. In the case of Irish La Tène objects:

> In this as in other cases, it is not always easy to separate La Tène and Roman forms, for the same Mediterranean ideas often underlie both.[22]

If the classification of objects found in Ireland as Roman is a problem, such classification is in several cases carried out using very restrictive criteria. J.D Bateson, in his major classification of Roman objects,[23] considers questionable all findings 'which might be Roman', including 'native copies of Roman types, or pre-Roman or post-Roman'.

If the same strict criteria were applied to a classification of Irish Celtic objects, the entire Celtic production would be decimated. A continuous flow of external influences shapes the uniqueness of the Irish objects. Yet nobody disputes that they are Irish.

Searching for pure *Romanitas* (as opposed to pure Celticism) in and around an empire which covered such a variety of people, cultures, traditions and artistic expressions, is wishful thinking. Not only did the borders of the Roman empire, in those years close to the maximum of its expansion, stretch from places as far away as Britain and Egypt, Dacia and Cyrenaica, Spain and Armenia, but it was an entity with a high level of internal mobility. Its army, just to cite an example, was a most heterogeneous one; a great carrier of new customs, religions and civil organisation. In Britain, 'Roman' troops included Spaniards, Germans, Gauls, Pannonians, Thracians , Africans, Dacians, Dalmatians and Syrians. Even beyond its frontiers the influence of the empire was enormous. Traders disseminated its goods and objects, its style of life, cults and language from India to the Sahara, from the Orkney Islands to the Caspian sea.

Most of all it was an empire deeply based on the idea of syncretism, the search for points of assimilation, rather than separation. It was an empire where differences were not eliminated but directed towards areas of convergence and where, therefore, the very concept of 'purism' had no room. It was this type of *Romanitas*, filtered through different channels and neighbouring cultures, that was slowly but decisively permeating Britain and, to a lesser extent, Ireland, in the first century AD.

Romano-British culture arose from the impact of the civilisation of Rome upon the Celtic people of Britain: the result, however, was not a replacement of cultures, but rather what can broadly be described as a synthesis ... At any one time, indeed, there was a wide range of variability within this synthesis, owing to the social stratification of Romano-British society on the one hand, and, on the other, to the varying conditions of life and opportunity existing in different regions of the province. At one end of the spectrum lay considerable approximation to the classical way of life and at the other a substantial survival of native characteristics. Moreover, the culture of Roman Britain should not be treated as if it were a static historical phenomenon.

Through the four centuries of its existence it had its periods of development and decline, of maturity and decay, despite the comparative slowness of such processes of change in the ancient world when compared with our own.[24]

The 'Loughey' burial must be seen in this cultural horizon, a Roman presence on the shore of Ireland where a landing was most likely to have taken place.

Most likely indeed, until on an undisclosed day of 1996 on the website: 'http://www.chestercc.gov.uk:80/chestercc/htlms/romans.htm' the following announcement appeared: *The other Irish question – A view from Chester*. Chester was officially putting forward its candidature as the alternative departure site of the first Roman invasion.

And not without reason. The fortress of Deva was built around AD 79 and immediately provided with harbour facilities. It is significant that the first garrison of Deva was the Second Legio Auditrix, which had been raised barely a decade earlier from the naval fleet based at Ravenna. Even more significant is the fact that the construction of the new fortress had been promoted by Agricola and that, during his governorship, Deva became the chief western legionary Roman fortress in Britain. Was Agricola's purpose to secure a key position to retain control over the just-subdued tribes of Wales and guarantee the defences of the northern frontiers, or had he something else in mind?

A large rectangular area of approximately 600 by 400 metres, the fortress is nearly ten acres bigger than a regular legionary fortress of around 50 acres. It could be that additional troops were located there for a special mission, possibly an invasion of Ireland? A clue is given by one inscription from the series in the fortress which seems to refer to a sailor rather than to a soldier and has consequently increased speculation as to the presence of a naval squadron, in addition to legionary forces, in the fortress.[25]

Altogether, there was a particularly large fortress, a military contingent with a maritime background and a harbour conveniently located at the mouth of the river Dee (hence the name of Deva for Chester) ideal for seaborne operations. This was the place from which all the English expeditions to Ireland set sail from the twelfth century onwards. One could reasonably wonder if these later expeditions were a replica of earlier Roman voyages. The answer is to be found on the east coast of Ireland facing the Deva fortress. Only if more signs of a Roman presence are identifiable in this area rather than in the north-east around Belfast, can Chester make a strong case for its candidature as the departure site.

To address this problem reference must be made to three fundamental works on the distribution of Roman material in Ireland: an article by F. Haverfield in 1913;[26] one by S. Ó Ríordáin;[27] and the edited article by J.D. Bateson in 1973.[28]

Haverfield, providing the very first list of Roman coins and objects from Ireland, notes that the great majority of finds come from the coast and their neighbourhood, that not all the coastline is represented but only the littoral from around Lough Foyle in the north to a point somewhat

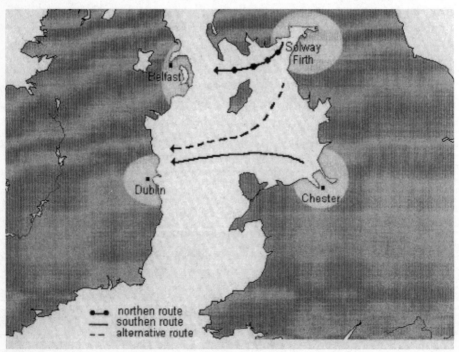

Map 2. First invasion departure and landing sites.

south of Dublin in the east. The material he is able to present is, however, so scarce (24 finds only are reported) and so biased in terms of the prevalence of finds of coins, that he cannot stop himself from commenting: 'If we were to confine our view only to the quite certain examples, it would seem as if Roman remains were almost as rare in Ireland as Solinus declared the snakes and the bees to be. This is partly due to neglect: modern Ireland cares little for ancient Rome.'

The situation had greatly improved 30 years later. Ó Ríordáin identified 60 find locations and three major cluster areas: the north-east of the country, the Dublin region and the Cork region (but here the bulk of the material is of a later date). While decisively confirming the legitimacy of both the Dublin and the Belfast regions as contenders for being the first Roman landing sites in Ireland, Ó Ríordáin's compilation was of little help in deciding which of the two should be given the title.

J.D. Bateson was actually in search of something else. He was pursuing his academic 'obsession' for pure *Romanitas* in Irish findings. This obsession has already been criticised for its lack of understanding of the variety and complexity of the Romano-Hibernian relationships. For once, however, such an obsession proves useful. If searching for the landing site of a Roman invasion we should be looking primarily for material with strong Roman connotations, of a type that Roman occupying troops would be likely to bring with them in war. Now Bateson provides us not only with a selection of this type of material (what he calls 'accepted findings') but also with a map showing its distribution in Ireland in the first and second centuries. The map indicates a maximum concentration of Roman material (140 finds altogether) in the Dublin region, thus providing important, though indirect, evidence in support of the Chester case.

Based on such evidence, we can comfortably look at the Dublin region as the most probable landing site and, though with much less comfort, to Chester as the likely departure site of the Roman expedition to Ireland. A short trip would be sufficient for the attacking troops. They would disembark in Ireland within a day or slightly more, depending on the departure and landing sites and on sea conditions. But what about the composition of the invading force? Romans? Celts under Roman

23

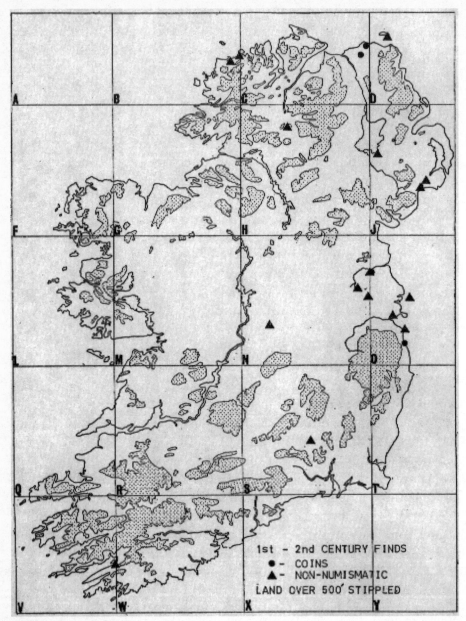

Map 3. Roman findings in Ireland.

command? Celts escaping the Roman domination in Britain? Or Celts operating autonomously but as Roman allies and with Roman support?

THE INVADING FORCE

These are all possible options. The most likely, because of its consistency with normal Roman practices in the region, is the one mentioned by Agricola to Tacitus: a mixed expeditionary force of Roman and auxiliary troops. Auxiliary troops, which certainly included soldiers of Celtic origin from Britain or other parts of the empire, were taking over the major role in open battle. Although previous examples of exclusive use of auxiliary troops in battle, with Roman troops backing them and intervening only when necessary, could be mentioned, it was Agricola who first introduced it as a deliberate practice within the Roman army to the point where Roman troops were progressively excluded from first-line field operations.

It is also quite possible that Romans used allied troops from the region, including expatriates from Ireland, to launch exploratory attacks on the island or to precede them in the case of a massive Roman attack. This is also a practice confirmed by Tacitus when mentioning that Agricola was on friendly terms with an exiled king from Ireland, hoping to make use of him should the occasion arise.

That phrase has inflamed the fantasy of some Irish experts. By linking an improbable mix of Irish legend and Roman history, and re-reading archaeological evidence with Celtic eyes, they have tried to transform a Roman invasion into an Irish invasion and an event of external domination into an internal affair.

The operation clashes with the reality of Romans using and manipulating allies (*divide et impera*) but never allowing them to take the control of strategic decisions or of key military operations. There is, however, one case in which the author manages to combine imagination and evidence into a sensible story, unlikely to be true, but certainly fascinating.

This is the story of Tuathal Techmar as told by R.B. Warner in his beautiful article which appeared in 1995 in *Emania*, the bulletin of the Navan Research Group. Tuathal Techmar's myth frequently appears in Irish legends from the ninth to the seventeenth century:

He is represented as a royal exile, originally from Ireland, who returned from Britain with an army to regain his right and kingdom. He was the ancestor of the Goidels, the last ethnic group to enter Ireland in pre-Christian times according to the medieval scholars. He defeated the other Irish tribes in a number of battles, some named, imposed a tribute to the Laighin and carved out a kingdom in the east midlands known as Mide.[29]

The date of his return to Ireland is indicated in the *Annals of the Four Masters* – a famous chronology of Irish events compiled in the seventeenth century – as AD 76. This is a coincidence of both circumstances and dates with Tacitus' story. Warner suggests that 'Tacitus confirms the Irish tale'. Should it not be the other way around?

In either case material evidence is needed, and Warner guides us on an archaeological voyage of Ireland in search of traces of the Tuathal (Roman?) invasion. The first site is a burial place in Lambay, a small island facing the County Dublin coast. Here, in the early 1840s, a Roman coin was found which has in the meantime been lost. A second discovery, some time before the 1860s, involved a decorated gold band and a sword. The sword is also lost, while the band, similar to other golden strips from British sites, has been attributed to the second half of the first century AD. A third main discovery occurred in 1927, on the occasion of works undertaken in the island harbour, with many objects found in association with crouched burials. The graves were immediately destroyed by the excavators and the objects passed from hand to hand before some eventually reached the National Museum, twenty years after their discovery.

When they reached the museum they consisted of a beaded bronze collar, eight rings of various size and material, five bronze *fibulae* or brooches, three bronze scabbard-mounts, many sheet bronze fragments, as well as a mirror and an iron sword which are apparently now missing. The iron sword was photographed before being sent, and never returned to the then technical assistant of the museum: it would appear, from the photograph, that the sword is not of Irish size and type. The *fibulae* are absolutely Roman. As to the fragments, they have been assembled into a disc, a triangular plaque and a bronze shield with suggestions that some of the remaining ones could be part of a crescentic plaque. All these objects have parallels in British or continental objects of the second half of the first century AD. According to Rynne, they also have a clear military application.

> It would seem reasonable to regard all the above sheet-bronze objects from Lambay as being very closely related, perhaps all from the same grave. Their association including a shield-boss, and the fact that close parallels for them can be found in other shield associations, strongly supports Macalister's suggestion[30] that the decorated disc might have ornamented a shield, and perhaps the triangular and crescentic plaques served similar purposes.[31]

Among the most unique and significant discoveries in Ireland, the objects from Lambay show a decidedly foreign character, a provenance from a heavily Romanised milieu, a prevalent military destination and a dating which is perfectly in line with the timing of a possible invasion of Ireland by Tuathal's forces. They confirm the theory of the Dublin region as the landing site for that invasion and the fact that they have been discovered in a harbour is also significant in this respect. Their association with a burial site puts them among the most reliable archaeological sources in Ireland. It is a great pity they were dealt with in this manner.

The voyage of Warner in search of Tuathal's passage continues to the sacred hills of Tara; the ritual capital of the Laigin at Knockaulin, near Kildare; the site of his last battle near Lyle Hill, County Antrim; and the hillfort at Clogher, County Tyrone. He finds early Roman material in all locations. Not much was found, but what was is extremely significant for understanding the importance of the relationship between Romans and Ireland at that time: '... while the quantity of the material is not large in itself it outnumbers any native Iron Age material from those contexts.'

There is another site, also mentioned by Warner, where important finds have been discovered that could bring further light to that relationship. But these finds have been seized and surrounded by mystery. The site is in Drumanagh at Loughshinny, twenty kilometres north of Dublin.

The mystery of Drumanagh
It all began with an article in *The Sunday Times* of 21 January 1996, which triggered a dispute of amazing bitterness. The initial sentences of the article are a bombshell:

A nondescript patch of land fifteen miles north of Dublin has shattered one of Ireland's strongest myths. It indicates that the country was, after all, invaded by the Romans.

For centuries its people believed it never happened. While Britain bent to the Roman yoke, the Irish were held to have lived in an heroic Celtic twilight on the fringes of the empire. There were no references in classical literature to a Roman presence in Ireland and when artefacts were found they were said to be imported.

Now archaeologists have revealed one of the most exciting Roman discoveries of the century. From beneath the soil at Drumanagh, clear evidence has emerged of a Roman coastal fort of up to 40 acres. It extends the known limits of the Roman empire.

The discovery has delighted archaeologists in Britain and Ireland and ends the established belief that Ireland remained free of Roman influence.

If not delighted, some were certainly impressed by the discovery. According to the article this was the case with Raftery, professor of Celtic archaeology at University College Dublin who is reported as saying that 'in his field of study the find ranked as the most important in Ireland'; with R.B. Warner, keeper of antiquities at the Ulster Museum, allegedly declaring that 'the excavation of the Drumanagh site would be the most significant excavation ever envisaged for any period in Irish history'; and Cunliffe, Professor of European Archaeology at Oxford University, who is reported as having described the find as 'staggering' and having said: 'It is one of the most important Roman sites in Europe and fits in exactly with what Rome was doing along all the frontiers of its empire.'

Others, however, were far from being delighted. The day after the article in the *Sunday Times* M. Herity, emeritus Professor of Archaeology at University College Dublin, expressed, in *The Irish Times*, his doubts over the recent 'discovery' and insisted that Drumanagh and the artefacts discovered there were most likely due to Celtic trading with Roman Britain: 'The story has been fantasised and blown up into something it's not.'

The immediate reaction of J. Maas, one of the co-authors of the original article, was printed in *The Sunday Times* the following week: 'Long-held ideas die hard and painfully and it would indeed be a pity if, in the fallout of academic rivalry and backstabbing, the huge importance of Drumanagh becomes merely a sideshow.'[32]

In the meantime the controversy was quickly spreading on the Web and was being re-fuelled by the press all around the world. It was even taking on political connotations. G. Cooney, editor of *Archaeology Ireland*, wrote : 'An editorial in *The Times* of London suggested that the Irish should not be ashamed that they were part of the Roman imperial world and that in this they were brothers as well as rivals of the British. There is a clear suggestion here that it really is time the Irish accepted the fact that they really are British. Within this new mythology it does not take too great a leap of the imagination to see how such a formulation could be used in political agendas today.'[33]

It was time to put water on the fire. Raftery tried to solve the dispute with a gently dismissive statement: 'Journalists, of course, have to sell newspapers and are, as is well known, generally at the mercy of their headline writers. They write under pressure and are not subject to the sort of rigid constraints of proof and logic which is expected of academic writings.'[34] It did not work. The reaction was one which did not leave space for conciliation.[35]

Warner tried a different way of finding compromise among the different fields: 'Perhaps the problem has been exacerbated by the use, in the recent publications, of the terms *Roman* and *invasion* which are popularly, but wrongly, equated with Italian (or at least Latin-speaking) and conquest respectively. Roman is a shorthand for anyone who lived (not necessarily originated) within the Roman empire and was therefore subject to Roman authority ... Invasion means military intervention on a scale rather larger than a raid. It does not necessarily imply conquest ...[36] With similar intentions, other diffusive arguments were proposed, for instance, suggesting that: 'It is possible that Agricola, in AD 83, tried to invade Ireland but was unsuccessful'[37] or by stating that 'In the absence of detailed assessment of the Drumnagh evidence it must be asked whether the whole question of Ireland's connection or relationship with the Roman Empire could or should be decided on the presence of any one site in Ireland. The answer is surely no.'[38]

Submerged in the mist of all these arguments, the issue of 'Drumanagh' has, in the meantime, been lost. Several years after the appearance of the article in *The Sunday Times* the controversy has been soothed, but the mystery of the site is still not unveiled. It is perhaps time to let facts talk and to bring back to reality, using the available evidence, the debate on this issue.

To put things in the right context it is first important to examine the very way the discovery of the site was carried out. The archaeological site of Drumanagh has been known for half a century. Already in the 1950s farmers plowing in Drumnagh had found fragments of Roman Samian ware. Those fragments never reached the National Museum and, as elegantly put by Bateson, 'their whereabouts are unknown'. In the 1970s, on the occasion of further deep plowing, more Gallo-Roman Samian ware was discovered, this time with professional archaeologists taking part in the exercise.

In the years which followed no organised excavation was undertaken but rumours spread among the archaeological community that the site was rich with important material and that this material was of 'easy' access. However, the rumours reached another community – treasure hunters. Instead of a scientific excavation, a wild pillage took place. In the mid-1980s Drumanagh was looted without mercy by people equipped with the most sophisticated metal detectors whose only purpose was to secure the largest possible booty. It was only then that the Commissioner of Public Works put a preservation order on the site. The landowner contested this as far as the Supreme Court but lost the case.

In the meantime, the material had disappeared only to reappear some time later at Sotheby's in London where the looters had tried to sell it. Eventually the finds were recovered and deposited in the National

Museum in Dublin. Since then, as essential evidence in an eventual prosecution against the illegal finder, the material has been seized and remains apparently inaccessible. The *Los Angeles Times* went as far as talking of 'a tale of state secrecy and scholarly sniping'.[39]

Behind legal technicalities and sharp comments lies the reality that Drumanagh has been for too long forgotten despite the evident interest in the site and the fact that the existing finds have been unavailable to the scientific community for far too long. If misinterpretations and exaggerations have proliferated, this is almost entirely due to the perpetuation of a situation of this type. The sooner the finds are disclosed and a full excavation of the site takes place, the sooner speculation will cease.

What is certain at this stage is the extraordinary importance of the Roman finds at Drumanagh. Raftery, one of the leading authorities in this field and probably one of the few who has had access to the material, comments:

> The Drumanagh promontory fort has clearly produced a collection of material of outstanding archaeological significance. This is certainly not an issue. Equally, it is not an issue that the material recovered indicates an overwhelming Roman presence on the promontory in the early centuries AD.[39]

Such presence is not limited to the promontory. The entire area surrounding Drumanagh and the larger Leinster region are scattered with Roman finds of the same period. We have already seen the vicinity of the military burial in Lambay island. We will talk of another military burial in Bray Head, just a few miles south of Dublin and, further south in Kildare, of the beautiful finds of yet another Roman burial. We already know, from the story of Tuathal Techmar, of the Roman material found in Tara, known to be important but still undisclosed almost fifty years after its excavation. We will talk later of the Samian ware and toilet articles excavated in Lagore, County Meath, and of the gathering of Roman coins at Newgrange.

The position of Drumanagh confirms the uniqueness of the site. The Drumanagh promontory fort was conveniently located on one of the most frequented routes in the Irish sea. The Ptolemy map clearly indicates that this area was well known to Mediterranean traders and travellers. Three centuries later, on his way north, St Patrick made a stop on the neighbouring island of Holmpatrick, opposite Skerries. Drumanagh was, altogether, an ideal landing site for an invading force.

The fact that available evidence has not been disclosed makes further argument difficult. However, one thing that cannot be easily hidden is the configuration of the Drumanagh fort, which so closely resembles other Roman forts of the invasion period in Britain.

On the shores of Kent, the Roman fort of Richborough was probably the first base of the Roman invading force. Its date can be definitely assigned to the reign of Claudius and its purpose was undoubtedly to cover the disembarkation of his legionaries and their war material at the time of his invasion of Britain in AD 43. The form of this fort definitively recalls the Drumanagh fortress as does the defensive earthwork, consisting of two ditches, which clearly resembles the multivallate defence of Drumanagh.[41] Even more impressive are the similarities between Drumanagh and the hillfort of Hod Hill in Dorset, bombarded by the Roman artillery and conquered during the invasion, as shown in Figure 1.

Drumanagh is a fort closely resembling Roman forts of an 'invasion' type, with an overwhelming Roman presence in the first and second centuries AD, located in the most likely landing site for an invasion and in an area scattered with Roman finds. Can we still talk of a mystery?

MATERIALISING THE INVASION

The burden of proof lies with the plaintiff, states a fundamental legal rule, and there is no reason why this should not apply to the hypothesis of a Roman invasion of Ireland. Evidence, however, is of two types: direct and circumstantial. When relevant and conclusive, circumstantial evidence has the same value as direct evidence.

Direct evidence for the invasion is certainly lacking. As far as we know, no contemporary writer has reported a Roman invasion of Ireland. Nor is Ireland crossed by Roman roads or marked by the presence of Roman walls or villas. Circumstantial evidence, instead, is overwhelming.

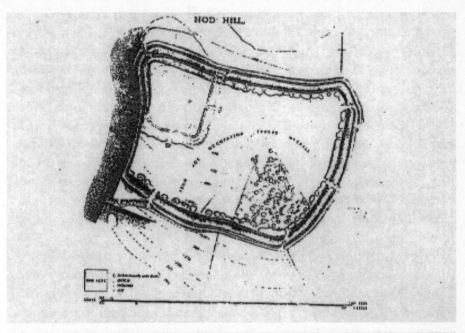

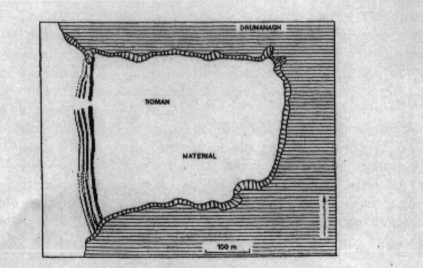

Figure 1. Two forts compared – Hod Hill, Dorset, Britain (top) and Drumanagh, Ireland (bottom).

We have seen how, in the second half of the first century AD, all the necessary preconditions for the launching of an invasion were in existence: an expansive imperial policy in the region; the strength and the success of the Roman army in Britain; the fortification of the coastal areas facing Ireland from which a seaborne operation could be started. We have also seen how Agricola was the perfect catalyst to transform such preconditions into real action and make the hypothesis of an invasion a fact. Finally, we have considered the archaeological traces of the invasion: contemporary burials of soldiers wearing their Roman arms; a fort, also belonging to the same period, greatly resembling other Roman invasion forts in Britain, spread with important Roman finds; and, scattered all around Ireland, but particularly in the areas surrounding the fort, a substantial quantity of Roman objects.

This evidence is certainly relevant. Both the historical context, on the Roman side, and the location of and interrelationship among various finds, on the Irish side, strongly support a reading of such evidence in terms of a Roman invasion to Ireland. Based on this important body of evidence, the assumption that an invasion indeed took place appears extremely convincing.

The invasion did not lead to a permanent conquest of Ireland but was certainly more than an occasional reconnaissance or a simple retaliation raid. There is no reason to believe that it terminated in a defeat nor that it was carried out by troops other than Roman, including, of course, auxiliaries. It is highly probable that the invasion took place in AD 82 or in the years which followed. The departure site was possibly located in the Stanwicks or in the Chester area, with the landing site in the Belfast or, more likely, in the Dublin region.

This first invasion was probably not the only one. Later Roman material and burials strongly hint at the possibility of at least a second invasion in the third century, probably leading to the establishment of Cashel, County Tipperary, whose name apparently derives from the Latin *castellum*.

CHAPTER 2

Roman Fashion in Celtic Ireland

MAKING PURPLE DYE

The Irish Sea can be very rough off the western shores of the Mullet Peninsula in County Mayo. The inhabitants of the Inishkea Islands, a granite, semicircular constellation of small pieces of land running parallel to those shores, used to be beaten by appalling winter storms with many lives lost to the fury of the sea. The last tribute was too much. After a drowning tragedy in 1927, when ten fishermen in curraghs were lost, the two islands of Inishkea North and Inishkea South were finally abandoned. Duvillaun More, further south, had already been abandoned at the turn of the century. Nowadays the islands are a diving paradise inhabited by geese (*Inis Gé* means Island of Geese), seals, snipes and corncrakes. The whales, hunted for centuries in these waters, can still be recognised, while passing in the outer sea.

However, these islands have been inhabited from very early times.

It seems certain that many centuries ago the islands must have been larger, and many of them were probably connected together, the two Inishkeas forming, for example, a single block. As a consequence they, and the opposite mainland, would have been less beaten by the waves and much more fit for human habitation. This would explain the great quantity of remains with which they are covered, ranging from rough megaliths and probable Bronze age sites to early Christian monasteries. We are not dealing here with a bare rock, a wild retreat of hermits as in the case of the Skelligs, but with islands which are still partly covered by a rich crop of grass, are surrounded by excellent fishing, and which, as well as the neighbouring peninsula, must have been at one time much more desirable for human habitation than the boggy country beyond Blacksod bay.[1]

To study this rich past Françoise Henry, a French scholar and one of the leading authorities in early Christian Irish art, conducted three archaeological campaigns in the Inishkeas. In her last campaign, in Inishkea North in the summer of 1950, she made an unexpected discovery: a wooden hut used as a workshop for the production of purple dye. In excavating the hut a considerable heap of several hundred *purpura* shells was found, mixed with some flat stones and pebbles cracked by the action of the fire. These must have been used for bringing to boiling point a liquid into which they were thrown. In the hut, a clearly defined part of the floor was covered by sea-sand with a strong salt content.

Purpura shells, water, fire and salt are all that is needed to produce purple dye. The molluscs were first pressed, mixed with salt or simply sea water and dried under the rays of the sun for three days in order to separate the juice from the body. The juice was boiled in water for ten days, skimming the liquid until it was reduced to half of the initial juice. Then the linen or woollen clothes were immersed and exposed to the rays of the sun. Was this process really carried out in the Inishkea hut, and was the purpose of producing purple there really targeted at dyeing clothes?

A survey of the plan of the Inishkea house, with a pit, a cellar, the remains of sea-sand and a hearth leaves little doubt as to its use. The pit in the west room was probably the place where the shells were crushed. The cellar must have been intended to keep the live fish or to hold the pulp while it was soaking with salt. The sea-sand to the north-west is probably beach-sand with a strong content of salt which could be used to the same effect. The large hearth can be explained by the necessity of keeping a fire constantly going for ten days or so.

The second question, about the destination of the purple dye produced in the hut, involves a less clear-cut answer. Given the crudeness of the process of extraction and the relatively small quantities of *purpura* found in the hut, Françoise Henry suggests that the final product is likely to have come out of the Inishkea factory in small quantities, which would be better adapted to the painting of manuscripts than to the dyeing of large fleeces of wool.[2] In the hut itself there is, however, a definite indication that the purple was primarily used for the dyeing of yarn rather than for manuscripts. Scattered in the hut are the remains of the working of chlorite, a soft stone extensively available on the island. There are also spindle-whorls at various stages of fabrication, many of them obviously split in the attempt of drilling a hole. A complete spindle whorl made of chlorite was found in another house on the island.

Here, on the shores of this remote part of Ireland, some time in the seventh century AD according to the excavator, people were producing and dyeing woollen clothes with purple. It was the point of arrival of a long process started thousands of years before on the Mediterranean shores.

DRESSING IN PURPLE

The Phoenicians had first discovered purple dye. Tyrian purple, for a long time, was the most celebrated of all dyeing colours, and possibly the first to be permanently fixed on wool or linen. The Phoenician colonisation of the Mediterranean was largely a matter of exploitation of this discovery. When the Mediterranean became *Mare nostrum,* the Phoenician factories continued to be exploited by the Romans. Rome's infatuation with purple dye grew in parallel with the increasing refinement of life and customs. In imperial times laws had to be issued to contain the use and abuse of this new fashion. Progressively, purple became a distinctive sign of rank in society and Roman magistrates used to mark their status by a purple band on their *tunica,* a narrow band for the equestrian order, a large one for the member of the Senate. As a symbol of authority, purple, was assimilated by the Roman Church: promotion to the purple is promotion to the rank of cardinal.

> It is for this colour that the fasces and the axes of Rome make way in the crowd; ... it is this that distinguishes the senator from the man of equestrian rank; by persons arrayed in this colour are prayers offered to propitiate the gods; on every garment it sheds a lustre, and in the triumphal vestment it is

to be seen mingled with gold. Let us be prepared then to excuse this frantic passion for purple, even though, at the same time, we are compelled to enquire, why it is that such a high value has been set upon the produce of this shellfish, seeing that while in the dye the smell of it is offensive, and the colour itself is harsh ... strongly resembling that of the sea in a tempestuous state.[3]

Most importantly, Romans exported the use of purple across their empire. Bright colours were much liked and used in the Celtic world, and purple dye must have been easily assimilated. Ireland would not have been the exception.

There is abundant evidence to show that bright colour abounded in clothing in early Ireland: this is especially the case with the 'brat' [mantle] which is generally described as being of a definite colour, though often with fringes or a border of some other shade. Purple or crimson and green are perhaps the commonest colours mentioned.[4]

Was this an early transfer then? But how early? Was it through the Roman Church or at an earlier date? The Mullet peninsula and its outer islands which look nowadays so isolated were, from the fifth century onwards, a flourishing centre of Christian expansion. Recent research indicates that St Patrick spent considerable time in County Mayo where, in AD 441, he remained 40 days and nights on the summit of Croagh Patrick fasting and praying for the people of Ireland. From the middle of the sixth century onwards, hundreds of small monastic settlements were established around the country, including settlements out of the Mullet peninsula in Inishkea North, Inishkea South and Duvillaun More. In Innishkea North a number of carved stone slabs are said to relate to St Colmcille. It is, however, difficult to imagine St Patrick and his followers engaged in promoting the fashion of purple dye. The fashion is likely to have been the result of a slow process of progressive assimilation. This process almost certainly started before the collapse of the Roman empire.

The key to solving this chronological uncertainty is quite simple and lies in the word purple. The Irish word for purple (*corcra*) derives from the Latin *purpura*. The transformation of the **P** of *purpura* into the **C** of *corcra* is an indisputable sign that the borrowing from Latin into Irish happened at a time when the Irish were unable to pronounce the letter P. Similarly *pluma* (feather) became *clúmh* and *Patricius* was transformed into *Cothriche*. Later, when the Irish had learned to pronounce P, it was kept in the borrowing of Latin words. Thus *pax* became póg and Patricius now became *Padrig* (today *Pádraig*). This is why the Irish language has a paucity of words beginning with P. In Dineen's *Irish-English Dictionary* (1927), among the consonants, P has the least number of pages, namely 40, against 157 for C.

The change to P took place no later than the fifth century. If purple had been introduced at a later stage the Irish word for purple could not be *corcra*. Unfortunately for clarity, the fifth century is the century when both the Roman Empire collapsed and St Patrick evangelised Ireland. This has allowed a great deal of 'manoeuvring' around the subject. However, it should not be forgotten that the fifth century is just a final limit and that the transformation of *purpura* into *corcra* could well have taken place at an earlier period in time.

Among early borrowings a selected number of words of a secular nature have been identified that bear witness to pre-Patrician linguistic contacts between the Roman empire and Ireland, particularly in the areas of trade and the army. These are the key contact areas between the Celtic and the Roman world since early times. It is not surprising that such words were also introduced early in Ireland. *Corcra* belongs to this group of early borrowings and it has been suggested that these words were introduced into Ireland as early as the third century AD, and so could be regarded as of the Roman influence.

BEAUTY AND MAKE-UP
During the excavations in Inishkea North two bronze objects were unearthed: a brooch and a bronze handle, both with undoubted Roman connotations.

The purpose of the bronze handle has greatly puzzled the excavator. It is of a type very common in Roman pans but with two special features which make this interpretation difficult to accept. It is covered by a sort of lining of thin bronze fixed to it by a sticky substance and has two rivet-holes. The excavator suggests that this handle may have belonged originally to a bronze pan of a Roman type and that, having been torn from it, it might have turned into the handle of a mirror by cutting two rivet holes in it. This would explain both the lining and the rivet-holes: the lining may have helped to strengthen the joint between the two different parts of the object, mirror proper and ladder. The rivets would have fastened these two pieces together.

If its interpretation is correct, this discovery, dating from the first century AD, confirms the early presence of Roman mirrors in Ireland, as further shown by one of the same period from a heavily Romanised milieu found in Lambay Island described earlier. In both objects the same rosette motif appears.

This motif has a long story. It appears on Syrian pottery as early as the fifth millennium BC and in Ancient Egypt, symbolising the lotus flower. Progressively it extends to the entire Mediterranean area to become part of the Roman repertoire of decorative motifs. The possibilities and permutations of the intersecting circles are enthusiastically explored in Roman mosaic and may have heavily influenced Irish art. Other motifs, often considered to be exclusive to Irish art, also have associations with the Roman world. Palmettes, trumpet, triskele, interlace, ring-and-dots and scrolls, typical of what has been defined as 'Romano-Celtic art', are largely represented in Roman Britain and Roman Germany and are scattered across the Roman empire.

These emerging links fully confirm the multiple composition and syncretist mission of the Roman empire, the intensity of exchanges across different regions, and the influence of Roman culture well beyond the borders of that empire at dates much earlier than previously believed. From this perspective there is no place, as we have seen, for pure *Romanitas*. There is no place either for pure Celticism.

The building of a model of Celtic art and the identification of Ireland as the place where this model has been developed without interruption from La Tène directly into early Christian art has been a largely shared view for decades. This view is now strongly challenged.

> ... Recent thinking allows greater possibility of Roman influence on Celtic art and argues that there is very little evidence for 'La Tène' culture in Ireland ... This is hardly demonstrative of a flourishing tradition. Furthermore, there is no indisputable reason to insist that the 'tradition' was unbroken to the early Christian period ... A strong case can be made out in the present state of scholarly thought for the origins of Dark Age Celtic art lying fairly substantially in the Romano-British repertoire. [5]

This is not only the case of mirrors but also of combs and a great deal of other toilette and ornamental objects.

If mirrors were needed to satisfy an Irish love of appearance, combs were essential to make the appearance as dramatic as possible. Elaborate hair dressing and a wide range of unusual colours of hair were used to impress friends and enemies. Diodorus Siculus tells us that Celtic fashion included, among others, the smearing of hair with limewater and then pulling it back to the top of their head and over the neck to produce something like a horse's mane.

The best collection of Irish combs has been found in the Lagore (crannóg) near Dunshaughlin, County Meath. Here, in the years 1934-36, Hugh Hencken guided the famous Harvard Expedition in a series of campaigns leading to some of the most interesting and best documented discoveries in the history of Irish archaeology. This was part of an ambitious, timely project, involving other major excavations carried out at Ballinderry and Cahercommaun, which saw the unique combination of the skills of a top level multidisciplinary team and the full financial support of the Irish government. These were the years after the great crisis of 1929 and the government paid the entire cost of labour for these excavations as part of its unemployment relief schemes.

The crannóg, an artificial island constructed by driving piles into the mud of the lake and building it up with layers of peat, brushwood, stone, branches and other available material until it rose above the water level of water, was surrounded by a heavy palisade. It had been inhabited for

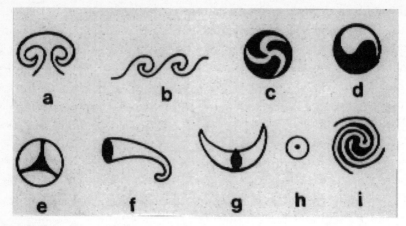

Figure 2. Decorative motifs in Romano-Celtic art: (a) palmette; (b) running scroll; (c) triskele; (d) ying-yang; (e) spherical triangle; (f) trumpet; (g) confronted trumpets; (h) ring-and-dot; (i) triskele spiral.

centuries, from around AD 650 to about AD 1000. Hundreds of objects were unearthed. Their classification and analysis took almost fifteen years to appear in a monumental report of more than 250 pages (a classic in this area) in the 1950 *Proceedings of the Royal Irish Academy.* Among these findings at least 50 bone combs and fragments were found that are latecomers in the chronology of the crannóg. However, as the excavator says '... almost every feature of its [Lagore] culture had come from outside Ireland within a thousand years before its founding by a slow but steady process of assimilation'.[6]

Within this process Roman influence played its role. The Lagore combs are classified as short, medium and long, the short type being the Irish version of the Roman and post-Roman Germanic comb.

Two of these combs clearly show the ring-and-dot ornament recurring in Roman objects. Late Roman combs often display this motif as in the case of the Iron Age hillfort of Lydney in Gloucestershire, re-occupied towards the end of the Roman period. Another comb shows a pattern of running spirals that will become the object of wonderful elaborations in later Irish art. Its source is, however, again the Roman ring-and-dot ornament where rings and dots are linked by connecting lines. In yet another comb interlace designs are present that most likely originated from the motifs of the rich and sophisticated mosaic production in late Roman Britain. Other Lagore toilet articles also display analogies with similar Roman objects (see figure 3).

The variety and quantity of Roman, Romano-British and Roman-derived toilet implements discovered in Ireland is remarkable. They are, in fact, among the most common small objects to be found on archaeological sites. At Freestone Hill, County Kilkenny, two nail cleaners of a type common throughout Roman Europe were found in an archaeological horizon marked by a Roman coin of Constantine II, dated AD 337-340, and by various artefacts of Roman inspiration. Possibly intended for the same use were other toilet implements characterised by a single hooked or claw-like plain end. One, found at Ballyness, County Donegal, has a twisted stem very similar to that of an ear spoon found in the Roman fort of Richborough in Kent, the stronghold, as we have seen, of Claudius' occupation of Britain in AD 43. Another was apparently found at Stoneyford, County Kilkenny, not far from a burial place of the second century AD that represents one of the most striking examples of permanent Roman presence in Ireland. The object is certainly Roman in type though the ornament appears to be of non-Roman workmanship.

Tweezers of Roman inspiration have been found in several Irish sites often in association with Roman material. One was found by H. Hencken when excavating Ballinderry crannógs in County Offaly together with a Roman melon bead and a piece of glass of Roman or sub-Roman type. He also found an article of this type at Lagore crannóg in a milieu strongly characterised by Roman traits.[7] Another pair of tweezers was unearthed at Garryduff, County Cork, and appeared to the excavator 'to have Roman origins' (see figure 4).[8]

Sometimes 'special' toilet objects were discovered. From a crannóg in County Meath comes an unusual toilet implement of Roman type described as a combined tweezers, tooth-and ear-pick. Another unusual but very significant find is a *ligula* from Knowth, County Meath, discovered in association with Samian ware of the second century AD. This is definitively a Roman object. A *ligula* is a spoon used for various purposes,

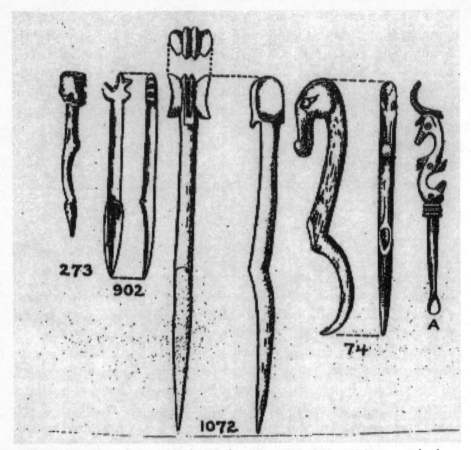

Figure 3. Roman influenced toilet implements: (273, 902, 1072) ear sticks from Lagore; (74) ear scoops from Lagore; (A) ear scoop from London.

especially to clean out small and narrow vessels and in particular for extracting cosmetics out of glass jars. The use of make-up was an extended practice among Celtic women and their way of making-up must have become very fashionable in Rome if the poet Propertius reproaches his mistress Cynthia for making-up in the way of the Celts.

This astonishing sequence of beauty objects not only confirms the paramount importance of personal appearance among the ancient Irish but also reveals a new picture of their interest in personal grooming. Like

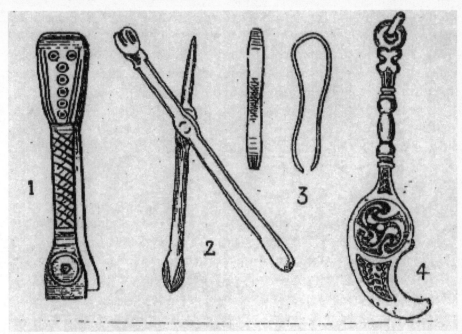

Figure 4. Toilet implements: (1) tweezer from Ballinderry, County Offaly; (2) combined tweezer, tooth and ear pick from County Meath; (3) tweezer from Garryduff, County Cork; (4) nail cleaner from Stoneyford, County Kilkenny.

the Romans they loved to bathe. They did it frequently (every day apparently) and used soap. According to Plinius, the Celts invented soap and transferred its use to the Romans.

It is a picture that strains and ultimately dissolves the myth of a primitive Ireland, isolated and substantially motionless in a golden age. It had been believed that in Ireland dramatic changes could only come from outside migrants or invaders, be these 'La Tène' or Celtic people. When mass migrations or invasions were difficult to prove on the basis of archaeological evidence, an alternative was proposed whereby small, but very determined, influential groups moved and established themselves in Ireland as new ruling classes – a situation very similar to that of the Spanish conquest of South America, where visionary conquerors with a few hundred men were capable of defeating and taking possession of large empires. This model could not, however, work within the Roman world. Romans never permanently conquered Ireland nor, given the nature, dimension and proximity of the Roman empire, could a discreet, élitist solution of the type indicated above be sensibly applied. Rome's influence and contacts with Rome were therefore simply eliminated from the Irish scene.

The model did not work well in the Irish world either. The attempt to find the origin of a unique Irish identity in this way backfired: an image of Ireland not only immaculate and untouched but also wild and uncivilised could not be sustained.

> They come to be portrayed, in a large negative and often sinister way, as the antithesis of the Anglo-Saxons, contrasting in all respects with the 'masculine' qualities of industry, imperial vigour and progress of the latter. The Celtic peoples, ancient and modern, were characterised as 'timeless' in this way, and widely seen as primitive insular Celts. It was also tacitly assumed that 'primitive' societies were fundamentally static and unchanging. The alleged characteristics of the Celtic 'race(s)' were associated with the famine, and with backwardness and inferiority; the Irish, particularly, were often viciously stereotyped as wild, dissolute, drunken and (probably worst) Catholic.[9]

This interpretative model has long been questioned but never fully discarded because, in fear of the 'Roman connection', scholars continue to make Ireland an anomaly rather than stressing its uniqueness in the long process of transformation from prehistory to history. It is time to definitively redress this anomaly. Something apparently marginal as personal grooming and personal ornament can be the starting point for such a reconsideration.

At the dawn of the Christian era, when Rome invaded *Britannia*, the Irish were far from being the primitive people described by early geographers and historians. They had long established links with the Mediterranean and the Roman world. They already shared with this world tangible and intangible features. Fashion and personal care were important elements of this commonality. It was a loose type of contact based on natural predisposition rather than enforcement or subjugation.

The Irish simply liked to have an impressive look and keep their bodies fit. Consequently, they needed mirrors and cosmetics, soap and dyes for their dresses, tweezers and combs, nail-cleaners and ear-picks. Some of these items they could produce themselves, others they found easier to import. In the Roman empire these items were already the object of mass production: inexpensive, delivered in a variety of forms, decorated according to the latest fashion. Now that Rome's borders were getting closer and closer, the opportunity was there to take advantage of the situation and to import from nearby markets what was needed and most liked. At the beginning this was a limited process, perhaps involving only the élite of the Irish population, but progressively it extended in importance and concerned a growing number of people. It required time. Ireland was beyond the borders of the empire. But *Britannia* was there, only a day's sail away, and traders could cross the Irish sea without difficulty. Eventually, trade, rather than armies, conquered the country.

Through trade Roman fashion and tastes, motifs and shapes, patterns and traits also penetrated into Ireland. A process of soft Romanisation took place. Roman objects and features became part of everyday life in Ireland and, in time, progressively became Irish objects and features. The necessary technology was increasingly available, workshops were created and local production began. It initially followed types and styles common in nearby *Britannia*. In the context of this, early production association with Roman material is not unusual and could even suggest that artisans from a Roman or post-Roman milieu were at the origin of these workshops.

The millenarian hillfort of Clogher, County Tyrone, had been inhabited from neolithic times up to AD 800. Here, in the fifth-sixth century AD, a furnace was in operation which is considered to be the place where ornamental metalworking in Ireland began.[10] Here too, brooches and a hand pin were found, which have their roots in the Roman metalworking traditions.[11] Most importantly, 31 shards of post-Roman pottery were found of a type belonging to the same period.[12] The progression from Roman to Irish design further developed in the centuries that followed. Irish production increasingly gained its own identity to bloom into the Irish Renaissance and a completely new original craftsmanship.

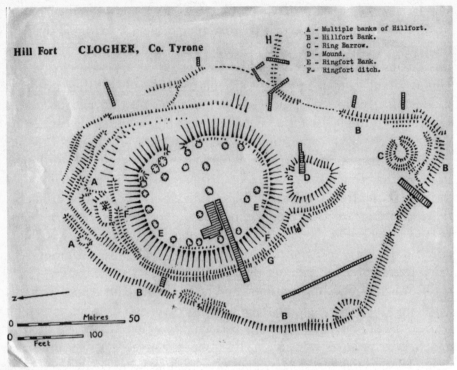

Map 4: Clogher hillfort, the cradle of Irish metalworking.

But the Roman roots are detectable for long to come.

A REVOLUTION IN PERSONAL ORNAMENTS
Personal ornaments fully confirm the breadth and importance of Roman influence. As we have seen, Romanisation was a long wave rather than just the result of occasional contacts, booty and military service. But the final impact was a revolution.

> By far the largest category of [Roman-influenced] material comprises items of personal adornment – penannular brooches, pins, rings, bracelets, dress-fasteners, combs and toilet articles. Collectively they may be seen as a revolution in dress, or at least in the adjuncts of it. There are, however, few areas of life that do not seem to have been influenced by Roman design.[13]

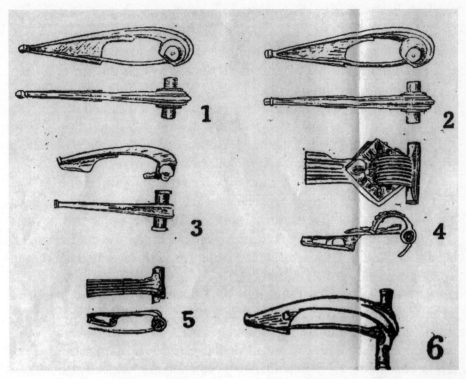

Figure 5. Roman fibulae found in Ireland: (1-5) from Lambay Island; (6) from Annesborough, County Armagh.

Brooches, pins and dress-fasteners of clear Roman inspiration 'invaded' Ireland and became an integral part of Irish fashion.

The Irish had, of course, their own designs for pins and brooches. As in other cultures, pins must have come first. In the second millennium BC the use of pins with a perforation in the head to hold a string to keep the pin in place appears frequently in a vast area spanning from Egypt to Troy, from Palestine to Cyprus, from Northern Italy to the Danube. In the excavations of Lagore, 132 pig-bone pins were found, many perforated, which witness the perpetuation of this type of pin many centuries afterwards in Ireland.[14]

Progressively, the thread was transformed to a metal string and the *fibula* was created. The Romans used the word *fibula*, from the Latin

49

verb *figere*, the same root of the English *to fix*, to indicate a brooch consisting of a pin and of a curved portion furnished with a hook. It was not, of course, only a Roman ornament. The *fibula* appears almost universally across the ancient world, particularly in the form of the safety-pin.

This story of evolution from pin to *fibula* is certainly useful in understanding the overall historical trend but in many cases, and certainly in Ireland, the reality appears less sequential and more complex. Metal pins, that had succeeded the bone pins, long coexisted with *fibulae* in different parts of the country, probably in response to different regional fashions.[15]

Most importantly, another story starts overlapping with the Irish one. The La Tène culture reached Ireland in the last centuries BC, bringing with it a number of new features from the Continent, and indirectly from the Mediterranean, that marked Irish personal ornaments and anticipated several traits of their future development. Zoomorphic elements in safety-pin *fibulae* are a point in case.

About two dozen La Tène safety-pin *fibulae* that originated in Ireland have been found. In several cases the foot section, into which the pin is fitted, has the form of a bird's head, and this is clearly continental in feature. Even a snake's head is represented in one *fibula*, though this type of reptile was unknown in Ireland. Inspiration and motifs clearly came from far away. Or was the fibula made by an immigrant craftsman?

When these *fibulae* were produced in Ireland, most likely at the turn of the first millennium, the La Tène style had ceased on the continent under the pressure of the expanding Roman culture. Little wonder that only a few years later, Roman *fibulae* made their entry into Ireland.

It is often assumed that Roman *fibulae* were the result of sporadic contacts with the Roman world through rare visitors and very occasional trade. This assumption is not likely to reflect reality. The number of Roman *fibulae* found in Ireland is around 25, equalling, if not exceeding, the number of Irish *fibulae*. They spread from as far north as County Donegal to as far south as County Cork, from as far east as County Dublin to as far west as County Galway. They cover the entire spectrum of centuries of Roman presence in Britain, from the first to the fourth. Altogether they witness much more than sporadic contacts, indicating a substantial opening of the Irish world to Roman motifs and objects.

Again, as in the case of La Tène *fibulae,* the entry of Roman *fibulae* to Ireland seems to be somehow delayed. Of five Roman *fibulae* found at Lambay Island one was of a type that had died out on the Continent by about AD 70, while another one had gone out of common use before the time of Claudius, in other words before the Roman conquest of Britain.[16] Unless we imagine direct contact between Rome and Ireland even before that conquest, the only logical explanation is that in Ireland, models of Roman *fibulae,* that had practically disappeared from the Continent, continued to persist.

This is true for another ornament that became progressively fashionable in Ireland: penannular brooches. These are a special type of round, annular brooch characterised by the fact that the ring is interrupted to allow the pin to swivel on the hoop. It was a brooch very popular all around the Roman empire from Britain to North Africa: women in the Maghreb still use it today.

The first type of penannular brooch that was fashionable in Roman Britain never reached Ireland.[17] Then, progressively, a few examples of later types appeared, one in Newgrange in a strongly Romanised milieu.[18] Later, a new type of penannular brooch appeared in Ireland which is characterised by terminals with motifs like heads, snouts, eyes and ears, hence the name of *zoomorphic.* Its origin is a mystery and its dating a puzzle.

Experts are much divided on this issue and the division reflects the sensitivity of the topic. We are no longer dealing with the Roman 'intrusion' of a minor ornamental object, rather we are questioning the very roots of Irish art as it will develop and flourish into the magnificent examples of the eighth century. If we only consider that the Tara brooch, one of the masterpieces of that art, is a *pseudo-penannular brooch* (pseudo, because the pin can no longer pass between the terminals of the hoop), with a variety of *zoomorphic* motifs, the importance of the origins of *zoomorphic penannular brooches* in terms of the uniqueness of Irish art and, eventually, of Irish identity itself, becomes immediately evident.

In 1937, H.E. Kilbride-Jones, a major authority in this area, wrote what was to become a significant classical reference work, 'The evolution

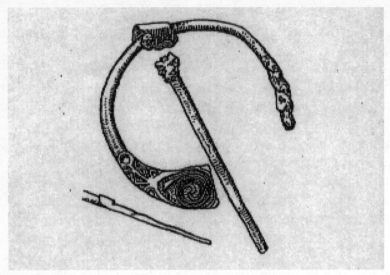

Figure 6. A penannular brooch from Clogher hillfort.

of penannular brooches with zoomorphic terminals in Great Britain and Ireland'.[19] He suggested that Roman types gave rise to Scottish zoomorphic penannular brooches and that these latter were the prototypes of the Irish ones; in other words, there was a Roman origin for this type of brooch. He was in excellent company. At around the same time two of the fathers of modern Irish archaeology, S.P. Ó Ríordáin[20] and J. Raftery[21] were proposing the same.

But the wind changed and H.E. Kilbride-Jones was devastated by criticism. More than 40 years later, in 1980, he is again on the scene with another major work, 'Zoomorphic Penannular Brooches', and still bitterly resents the treatment received:

Forty years ago an attempt was made at devising an evolutionary sequence for penannular brooches with zoomorphic terminals. The attempt was not entirely successful, and in the ensuing years critical appraisals have been published. Charges of eccentric thinking, even of partisanship, have been made. To this serious worker, the suggestion of partisanship is abhorrent.[22]

What was the cause of such acrimonious contention? According to the most extreme critics zoomorphic brooches had to be taken for what they were: an Irish invention owing nothing to anything that had gone before. And the dating of their appearance had to be moved from the mid first century to between the fourth and fifth centuries, which accommodated the fact that before the fifth century there is no conclusive evidence from Ireland of native ornamental metalworking,[23] and puts such appearance safely into the early Christian era. Eventually, a more balanced approach emerged based on the recognition that this type of brooch is part of the increasing cultural interplay between the two countries and that possibly some early examples already reached Ireland from Britain in the third century. Two unique objects confirm the importance of this interplay.

Twenty years ago, in the Temple of Sulis Minerva at Bath, a penannular brooch was excavated from the spring of naturally occurring hot water that lies at the centre of the temple and bathing complex. Here the Celtic and Roman cultures have met for centuries. Sulis was a Celtic goddess already venerated in this place probably for her healing powers associated with the beneficial properties of the water, which was equated to Minerva, the Roman goddess of handicrafts but also of the medical world (*Minerva Medica*) when the Romans arrived here in AD 43.

This was a special place where, on the outskirts of the empire, the Celtic religious tradition was perpetuated in a perfectly classical Roman environment. The votive offerings found here, including 12,000 coins, confirm that we are in a strongly Romanised milieu, to which the penannular brooch belongs.

It is an exquisite object. The terminals, inlaid with red enamel, bear zoomorphic ornaments. On the left there is a long-tailed bird looking over its shoulder at a plant, on the right another long-tailed bird above a fish. The form of the brooch compares exactly to a certain type of Irish zoomorphic penannular brooch. None of these, however, has representation images on the terminals, while the motif of a bird, and in some cases of a bird preying on a fish, occurs in Romano-British brooches and other Romano-British objects. Furthermore, the style of the animals is clearly rooted in the continental 'naturalistic' tradition rather than in the Irish tradition.

> Although zoomorphic penannular brooches are quite rightly regarded as being within the range of products made by Celtic craftsmen, nevertheless very few are decorated with typical Celtic art motifs.[24]

The presence of an object like this one, not in peripheral areas of northern Britain but in the highly Romanised Bath, clearly shows the pointlessness of all efforts aimed at clearly separating the Irish from the Roman ornamental world. It has been suggested that the Bath brooch is the work of a smith from the east of Ireland, though influenced by the art of *Britannia*.[25] More recent research suggests, however, that there is no real reason to presume that the brooch was made in Ireland, although it was obviously made by a highly skilled craftsman working in the same tradition as the smiths who produced similar pieces made in Ireland.[26] Due to great uncertainty about dating and provenance (more than one-third of Irish zoomorphic penannular brooches are unprovenanced), it seems only possible to trace a scenario of mutual influence with penannular brooches proliferating in the Roman empire, taking new inspirations in Roman Britain and moving to Ireland. Irish artistic influence had, in turn, a bearing on these and other provincial Roman artefacts in a continuous process of artistic refinement.[27] Eventually the process culminated in the emergence of a totally autonomous, new and unique, ornamental Irish style. Another, very peculiar find, confirms this interpretation.

An antler pattern book with four facets, each one representing motifs for the production of metal artcrafts, was found at Dooey, County Donegal. It includes multiple lozenge designs, the chevron pattern, spirals, single and double, and the marigold motif. These motifs were very popular in the Roman empire and in Roman Britain, in particular, during the first and second centuries AD. They are also, with the exception of the marigold, leading motifs in zoomorphic penannular brooches.

The close stylistic correlation highlighted by the Dooey find is not, however, also a chronological one. Again we witness a time lag between Romano-British and Irish objects. While the decorative style represented

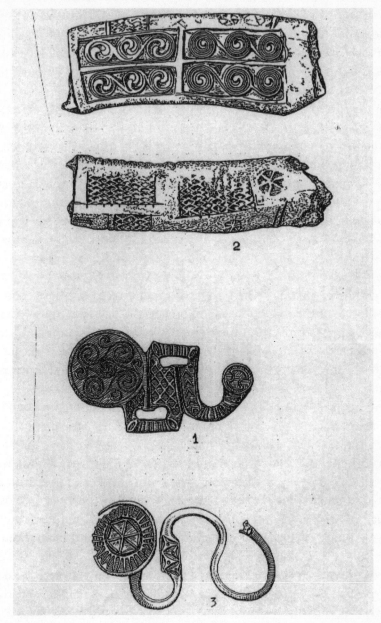

Figure 7. Irish ornamental latchets (1 and 3) and pattern book (2).

in such a find is typical of the first two centuries AD in Roman Britain, its appearance in Ireland is at least one century later if not more, and even much more, according to certain experts. The dating of the Dooey object reflects this uncertainty: it ranges from the third-fourth century to the sixth, or even seventh century, depending on attributions.[28]

But the interplay does not finish here. The latchet, a very special type of dress fastener with a disc-shaped head and an S-shaped body, which was attached to the dress by two wire coils, is usually considered, like zoomorphic penannular brooches, an exclusively Irish object. Difficult to imagine something more 'Irish' than this. However, its ancestor, a latchet brooch from Icklingham, Suffolk, with its stellate pattern and background of punched dots typical of the Roman decoration, belongs to the Romano-British milieu.[29] And, if we look at two of the most famous early Irish latchets (the ones from Dowris, County Offaly and from Newry, County Down) we again find the motifs of the Dooey pattern book: trellis, chevron and spirals on the first one and the marigold on the second. The marigold, one of the most universal motifs in the Roman empire, has here straight-cut petals typical, in their crude symbolism, of altars and tombstones erected by soldiers of the Roman army. One such altar is that dedicated to the god Vitiris by Tertulus in Chester.[30] Is not Chester one of the most accredited sites for a possible Roman invasion of Ireland?

Here again the time lag occurs since latchets are contemporary if not successive to zoomorphic penannular brooches. The same can be said of another 'typical' Irish object: the hand pin.

The original perforated bone pin had gone a long way. It had evolved into a variety of ring-headed pins whose inspiration can be traced in Roman Britain. In this context also originated, in the first and second centuries AD, rosette pins and later on, in the third or fourth century, ibis-headed pins which are considered the ancestors of the hand pin.

It was probably in Roman Britain that the proto-hand pin emerged out of such antecedents. Despite claims for an earlier origin in Ireland or Scotland, there is no real evidence that they were to be found in either area before the end of the fourth or the beginning of the fifth century.[31]

THE TIME LAG

The persistence of mutual inspiration, on one side, and of a recurrent time-lag, on the other, between the Roman and the Irish ornamental productions is a leitmotif that marks the distance-proximity of the two worlds. Taken from astronomy, we are in a part of the universe where the two planets (cultures) are within a visible distance from one another. They certainly do not belong, as sometimes argued, to different celestial spheres out of reach of mutual light signals or embedded in the invisibility of alternative spaces, such as in the case of 'black holes'. In our case, things themselves witness beyond doubt the richness, significance and depth of the interplay. And there is no need to imagine space vessels (rare merchants, a few soldiers, lost ships and the like) engaged in occasional, solitary missions from one planet to the other. This is an interchange that lasted for centuries, became increasingly important and deeply shaped the entire development of Irish culture.

La Tène *fibulae* reached Ireland when La Tène was at the very end of its history on the Continent. And, as we have seen, Roman ornamental motifs continued to develop and be popular in Ireland after they were out of fashion in the Roman world. It is somehow like when we look at the sky, at planets or stars, which no longer exist, but whose light eventually reaches us. The image of the Roman world projected into Ireland was for centuries a late one and continued consequently to exert its influence on the Irish world even after the collapse of the Roman empire. That is the reason why it is impossible to limit the influence of *Romanitas* on Ireland only to the period of the Roman settlement in Britain. This story spans the period up to at least the Viking invasion. Then, but only then, will the planet Ireland enter a different constellation.

CHAPTER 3

Roman Farming and Irish Ring Forts

FROM ROUND TO SQUARE

At the extreme outskirts of County Kerry, facing the ocean, the small town of Caherciveen totals only 2,000 souls. This is not, however, a place to be forgotten. Here O'Connell was born in 1775 and the ruins of his mansion are still there, a short distance away on the Glenbeigh road. The ruins of other houses, more than 1,000 years older, are also not far away.

Standing on a massive rock-eminence that commands Valentia Island and Dingle Bay, the stone fort of Leacanabuaile is one of many *cashels* spread throughout Ireland. It has, however, an extremely rare feature. When excavated in 1939 and 1940, the fort revealed the overlapping remains of several houses of different shapes, the main two houses being a round one, house A, and a square one, house B. It is not only a matter of shape. The square house is much bigger than the round house, almost double in internal space. Construction techniques are much more refined in house B with a roof most likely consisting of a thatched timber construction against the much simpler, exclusively thatch-based roof of house A. Only the square house is equipped with a covered drain dug into the clay to carry off water towards the eastward slope of the fort. Altogether an improvement in living conditions, still very basic but certainly different from the past.[1]

Most importantly, the way the two houses were built indicates without doubt that the square house was constructed after the round one: house B was built against, but not bonded into, the wall of house A. The Leacanabuaile excavations are the tangible proof of a major change in

58

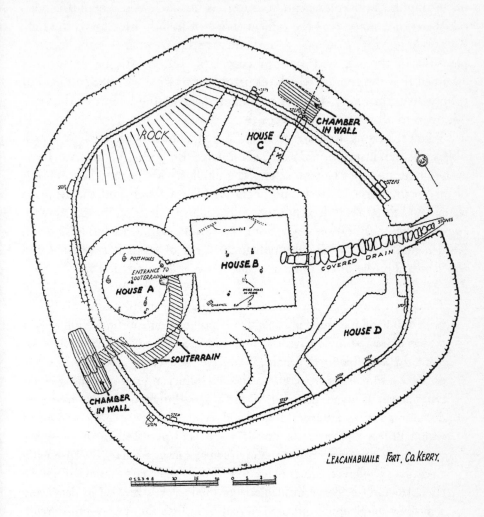

Map 5: Round and square houses at Leacanabuaile fort, County Kerry.

the way people were living in Ireland. But when did this major shift occur and what caused it?

The time span to be considered is very long and concerns the elusive Irish Iron Age period. We know for certain that, although rare examples of rectangular houseplans can be traced as far back as the neolithic period, the round shape was the typical shape of Irish houses up to the Late Bronze Age. More evidence with distinctive square shapes only becomes plentiful in the six and seventh centuries AD. It can be reasonably assumed that the change which occurred at this time was not sudden but progressive, thus very difficult to date and, given the length of the period, open to all sorts of influences.

Vikings, Saxons, Romans and the Church all have been invoked as possible sources of inspiration for the new square Irish house. Vikings are, however, out because they came too late. The similarity with Anglo-Saxon houses in Northumbria is far from conclusive. The Church and the Romans remain and these are indeed not mutually exclusive. In fact, Roman churches draw their inspiration both from the rectangular form of the Roman *basilica* and from the circular/polygonal form of Roman *hypogaea* and *nymphaea*. But the direct influence of Rome is quite a possibility:

> Though we should perhaps not expect to find Roman villas or similar structures in Ireland it is quite possible that British or Romano-British refugees or traders in Ireland could have used or introduced rectangular framed building. Similarly, Irish raiders in Britain could have copied simple Roman structure on their return if these were considered a sufficient improvement over the type current at home. Irish settlements in west Britain could also have produced some reflux influence. Round and rectangular houses have been found within British hillforts re-occupied in sub- and post-Roman times, so we would have no scarcity of sources of origin and inspiration for the Irish Early Christian period rectangular house were it not for the fact that in general the later structural evidence available from these sites is meagre in detail and sometimes ambiguous compared to that from Irish sites of seventh-eleventh centuries after the end of the Roman period.[2]

We face again the recognition of a likely Roman influence, which must be immediately mitigated by an insistence on the occasional nature of contacts between Ireland and Rome and then questioned by the argument that changes would have occurred after the end of the Roman empire. Both arguments are, as we have seen, inconsistent with the facts. Roman influence was a pervasive one and progressed through centuries into Irish culture in a continuous, rather than sporadic way. Due to the peripheral position of Ireland vis à vis the Roman empire, a time lapse of at least one century separated the history of the two cultures with the consequent projection of the influence of the Roman world well beyond the disappearance of the empire.

The issue, however, is much more simple and yet more complex than that. The shape of a Roman house was probably a source of inspiration for the Irish, but that this inspiration was the ultimate cause of change is another matter. Building a house in a different way means changing the roots of a culture. No one (certainly not the Irish) would carry out such a change for reasons of sheer imitation. Major, epochal events must have happened and marked the shift. We have to consider centuries of modifications in the Irish landscape to disentangle the matter.

THE RESURGENCE OF AGRICULTURE

When in the early 1960s Frank Mitchell and Hilda Parks extracted an 8-cm-long 'carrot' from the boggy soil near Littleton, County Tipperary, they could hardly imagine that this contained what is perhaps the most complete sequence of pollen records ever made available in Ireland. Spanning 12,000 years of Irish prehistory and history, the sequence shows the endless struggle between trees, bushes, herbs and human cultivation from the neolithic times to our age.

Bushes and trees dominate the scene in early millennia with the massive presence of hazel *(corylus)*, alder *(alnus)*, oak *(quercus)*, birch *(betulla)*, elm *(ulmus)* and ash *(fraxinus)*. Farming is a tiny presence until around 2,000 BC when the land starts being cleared and grasses *(gramineae)*, make their way together with cultivars *(cerealia)*. It is the beginning of agriculture centred on the exploitation of grassland on the one hand and of tillage on the other. The long process of progressive development of agriculture that started then was not, however, straightforward, periods of expansion were followed by 'retreat' periods with trees and shrubs regaining, sometimes in a very substantial way, areas previously cleared.

The most dramatic of all retreat periods occurs in the Early Iron Age, from about 300-200 BC to about AD 200-300. Almost all traces of weeds associated with agriculture, such as dock, thistles, sage and goosefoot vanish. Then pollen of cereals seems to fade away. It is what Mitchell calls a 'lull in agriculture', combined with general woodland regeneration in practically the whole of Ireland.

Suddenly, towards the end of this period, a new era opens. Cereal pollen starts increasing again and woodland begins an endless retreat. There will be no return. The start of an expansion period for agriculture begins that will never be seriously interrupted in future and will eventually culminate in its taking over the woodland and becoming the predominant feature of the Irish landscape. The shift witnessed by the few centimetres of soil that correspond to this period in Mitchell's 'carrot' marks the entire agricultural history of Ireland. But what caused this shift, and when did it happen? Mitchell explains:

A new phase of intensive farming opens about AD 400 ... Though the Romans never invaded Ireland, knowledge of their way of life and of their agricultural techniques certainly penetrated the country and gave rise to intensification. It was probably at this time that ploughs armed with iron coulters come into Ireland and that tillage becomes both easier and more rewarding. The spread of Christianity in Ireland and the establishment of large monasteries with their own farmlands will have hastened the rise in agricultural efficiency.[3]

Roman techniques were then at the origin of this major agricultural revival around the time of the arrival of Christianity in Ireland, according to the Littleton pollen records. Records from other locations fully confirm this general picture, but timing is not necessarily the same and it is sometimes 'anticipated' in respect of the Littleton dating. In other words, it may well be that Roman influence was exerted earlier, and therefore more directly, than originally thought.

Among the most important pollen sequences, the one collected at

Loughnashade, in the area of the Navan fort, shows trends that almost totally tally with the ones from Littleton. The agricultural revival starts here, however, as early as the first or second century AD in the period of full Roman expansion in Britain. Let the words of the scholar who first studied these pollen records speak for themselves:

> There is the crucial point of exactly what date the marked clearance and increase in arable agriculture, particularly at Loughnashade and Killymaddy and Weir's loughs occurred. There are quite marked fluctuations in the deposition rate at Loughnashade, matching changes in between agricultural and forested landscapes, and this makes estimation of dating somewhat more difficult. It would, however, appear that the initial increase in cereal pollen, and thus the proposed introduction of the arable agricultural system, began as early as *c.* AD 150-200, and was fully developed by about 300 A.D. This dating is certainly open to revision, but would fit quite well with one major line of archaeological evidence, the beehive quern.[4]

NEW TECHNIQUES

Two of the major new techniques leading to the revival of Irish agriculture in the early centuries of the first millennium have already been mentioned: coulter plough and beehive querns. Both have their origin in the Roman world.

The word coulter, a direct borrowing from the Latin *coulter*, was used to designate an iron blade that was fixed in front of the share of traditional scratch or light plough, the ard. The share itself started to be reinforced by an iron shoe. Later a mouldboard was added which turned the sod left or right, depending on how it was attached, and exposed much larger portions of the soil. These apparently minor improvements brought dramatic changes in Irish agriculture. It was now possible to cut the sod much more effectively than before and this allowed for the progressive abandoning of the traditional criss-cross ploughing. No more need for two passages to penetrate the tough grassland soil first and then break the ground with a second passage. With only one passage, and a reduction by half of the time needed, fields were ready for sowing.

The traditional form of what the archaeologists call the 'Celtic field', a square one imposed by the old technique, was replaced by all kinds of patterns that better match the irregular shapes of the Irish landscape. Different types of soil previously denied to cultivation, such as clay, became accessible to agricultural activities. A rational use of land progressively replaced the sporadic exploitation of previous ages.

Coulter ploughs were almost certainly borrowed from Roman Britain. More than 25 have been found in south-west Britain, in areas of high Roman influence. Within these areas three villas, three towns and at least three fairly substantial Roman civil settlements have produced coulters. Early examples date from the third century AD, with the large majority being late fourth century in date. One should be careful, however, with interpretations that are too facile. These were expensive objects and the large quantity of iron they contained made them valuable as scrap. Significantly, more than half of the plough coulters found in Britain belong to hoards of Roman ironwork.[5]

Their introduction in Britain is thus likely to pre-date the third century and possibly already occurred during the first two centuries of the Roman conquest. Similarly for Ireland, where no example of coulter plough has yet been found pre-dating the fifth and sixth centuries AD, it can be reasonably argued that their introduction occurred in earlier times. It was again a slow process. The material was costly and the new technique required the clearance of more fields from stones, a very time-consuming activity. A parallel, though more complex, history is progressively emerging for the rotary querns.

The dating of these querns is a matter of controversy among specialists, the question being: did they pre-date or were they contemporary with the Roman presence in Britain? Or, to put it more clearly: were they a Celtic invention or a Roman derivative?

There are two distinct forms of rotary querns. Flatter 'disc querns' and dome shaped 'beehive querns'. More than 100 beehives have been identified in Ireland, primarily from unexcavated places and almost exclusively concentrated in the north of the country. In Britain hundreds of beehive querns have been discovered on Romano-British sites, to the point that E.C. Coewen, who first attempted a classification of British beehives in 1937, identified as 'Roman Legionary' type the numerous beehive querns found in Roman sites in the northern frontier.[6]

The Roman legionary type has a bun profile, a cup or funnel shaped hopper, a narrow pipe perforation in the upper stone and an *unpierced* handle hole. These are characteristic features of the vast majority of Irish beehive querns.The similarities are further confirmed by the analysis of the diameter and thickness of Irish and north British beehives, the majority of beehives from both groups concentrating in the crossing area between 30cm diameter and 15cm thickness.[7]

There is apparently no way of dismantling this massive concurrence of common elements pointing at a Romano-British origin for Irish beehive querns. Still it has been tried. Since such querns are almost wholly confined in the northern half of Ireland and practically none have been found in association with habitation sites, there must certainly be a mystery and, to explain the mystery, a suggested solution. What about an immigration of Celtic people in the first century BC?[8] Why not propose that beehive querns were used for some unclear ritual rather than, as the poor layman would think, for grinding cereals?[9]

The real mystery is how, with the majority of beehive querns, the exact context of the find is not known. Why is the clear association between Roman material and beehive querns in Britain not given adequate consideration? Why is the fact that the distribution of beehive querns in Ireland coincides with one of the major areas of concentration of Roman material not properly recognised? Why, instead, is the idea of a Celtic invasion of Ireland proposed time and time again as the ultimate solution of everything despite the fact that it is largely unproved?

It seems almost heretical to insist that a Celtic invasion of Ireland never happened. In this regard, however, the archaeologist should bear in mind the deficiencies of the discipline. Perhaps, as in the field of religion, he should adopt a stance akin to that of the agnostic rather than one of outright atheism. Perhaps there was, indeed, a migration of 'Celts' to Ireland. The only problem is archaeology cannot prove it.[10]

There is no mystery at all. Roman agricultural techniques spread in Britain first, developed special features there and eventually entered the Irish scene already in the first or second century AD. A slow process of assimilation then started which intensified in the following centuries. Agriculture is a conservative area and is never immediately receptive to innovation. All around the Roman empire farmers continued to use the ard long after the coulter plough had been introduced. This led, in turn, to an agricultural revival in the third century which was further facilitated, but not initiated, by the incoming Christian monks' communities. Beehive querns are just part of this panorama. They witness the substantial appearance of cereals in Ireland and the domestication of Irish agriculture.

NEW PLANTS

In the better exposed soil, richer in nutrients, 'new' plants that were widespread in the Roman world could be cultivated, in a more permanent way. Romans had introduced wheat into Scotland[11], and wheat has been found in Lagore excavations in a context characterised by strong Roman connotations. Here as we have seen, pins and toilet articles of clear Roman inspiration were found but also axes, an adze and a fork together with parts of heavy ploughs and querns, all descending from Roman types.[12]

Rye pollen also appears for the first time in significant amounts in Ireland.[13] *Secale* is the Latin world for rye, *secal* in Old Irish. The words for spelt wheat and emmer wheat originate from Latin too: *sillechis* is a borrowing from Latin *siligo*, while *r´uadún* can be compared to the Latin *robus*. Other words borrowed from Latin clearly show how cereals were not the only 'new' crops to be introduced.

Lentils, broad beans, garden peas and chickpeas were typical of Roman cultivation. Only two of these vegetables, the broad beans and garden peas, were capable of standing the cold, humid climates and made their own way to Ireland. The Old Irish word for pea is *pis,* a clear borrowing from the Latin *pisum,* while the Latin word *faba* for broad bean is at the origin of the Welsh *ffa*, the Cornish *fav* [long a], the Breton *fav* and the Irish *seib.*

Similarly, the Irish word for cabbage *braisech* is a loan from the Latin *brassica,* and the word *foltchép* for chives contains the Latin word *cepa* for onion. Also the word for stubble *(connall)* comes from the Latin *cannula,* as do the Irish *súst* (Roman *fustis*) for flail, *saball stabulum* for barn, *sorn furnus* for an oven for drying grain, and *muillen molina* for mill.[14] New milling techniques, particularly the introduction of the water mill together with the introduction of the coulter plough and beehive querns, mark the passage of agriculture from a scattered activity to an organised one, the beginning of new processes that will change the entire way of living in Ireland.

NEW PROCESSES

Water mills *(molae acquariae)* had a long history in the Roman world. Five major writers – an architect, an historian, an agronomist, a poet and a bishop – describe the steady development of this revolutionary source of power along a period of more than six centuries. In the first century AD Vitruvius provides the first description of the new machine. A cogged wheel, attached to the axis of the water wheel, turned another wheel which was attached to the axis of the upper mill-stone: the corn to be ground fell between the stones out of a hopper which was fixed above them.[15] One century later Plinius in his *Historia naturalis*[16] mentions the water mill again but not as a very common device. Three more centuries will elapse until Palladius returns to the subject. In the meantime water mills have become well known and it is only a matter of encouraging a rational use of the water available for power:

> ... if you have a plentiful supply of water, the mill should receive the effluent of the baths, so that you may construct a water mill in that place, and have your corn ground without the labour of animals or man.[17]

They also progressively spread around the empire. In the fourth century Ausonius mentions their existence in the Ruwer near Trier. In the sixth century, Venantius Fortunatus, in describing a castle on the banks of the Moselle, makes distinct mention of a tail race, by which a tortuous steam was conducted in a straight channel, to activate a water mill.

One century later the Roman water mill reaches Ireland. The oldest one is dated by dendrochronology to about AD 630. The potential of the new machine is astonishing. The Vitruvian mill, and to some good extent its Irish successors, could grind forty times as much grain per day as the donkey mill, that is about 3.6 tons of grain per day.[18]

Subsistence agriculture is progressively replaced by more intensive, 'modern' types of agriculture, based on rational use of the soil, the introduction of a larger variety of crops and the use of much more efficient techniques and processes. This would in turn lead to a dramatic increase in food production, general well-being, and eventually to an increase in population. This trend was strongly reinforced by the introduction, at this time in Ireland, of the know-how and technology of dairying. This also came from the Roman world.

> The Romans were familiar with the technology of the production of butter and cheeses, and it was the introduction of this expertise to a country that has unquestionably the most suitable natural resources for the rearing of cattle in Europe that gave rise to the economic revolution outlined above.[19]

But when did this happen and how? The answer is to be found at the hill-fort of Dún Ailinne near the little town of Kilcullen, 30 miles from Dublin in County Kildare. Here, at the edge of the Irish central plain, the landscape is open grassland and large pastures, an ideal place for cattle farming. When the site was first excavated in 1968, within the large area of the complex (400m in diameter) 18,500 animal bones and fragments were found, the most extensive faunal assemblage of the Iron Age in Ireland. Cattle remains accounted for more than half of the total discovery and, when analysed, revealed that the majority belonged to very young calves or adult cows.

An apparently straightforward explanation was at hand. Pam Crabtree of Princeton University saw in these remains a clear indication of the primary use of cattle for dairy farming in Dún Ailinne. As she explains:

> ... calves must be produced each year to initiate lactation in cows. Since only

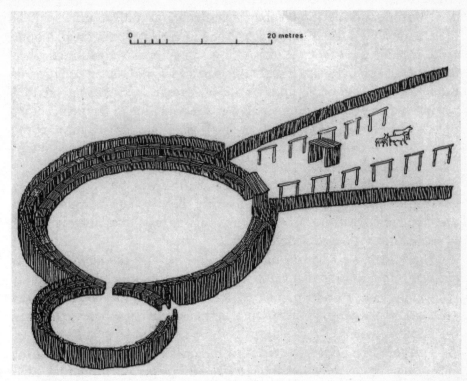

Figure 8. The keep of Dún Ailline, suggested reconstruction of the summit area.

a few bulls are needed for reproductive purpose, most male calves will be killed shortly after birth. This would explain the large numbers of neo-natal and young juvenile cattle seen at Dún Ailinne. Cows, on the other hand, are the productive members of the dairy herd. Most cows will not be slaughtered until their milk production declines, usually at relatively advanced stages.[20]

This interpretation would also have the advantage of being perfectly in line with the historical sources suggesting that cattle in ancient Ireland were kept primarily for milk rather than meat. Early Irish laws of the six and seventh century AD clearly indicate the paramount importance of dairy farming in Irish society. This was a society where milk cows were the common unit of currency, where the position of the individual in the community and the value of the land were determined by the number of cows and where

69

dairy-herding was much more important than crop cultivation.[21]

Had it always been so? If Crabtree's interpretation of Dún Ailinne cattle remains is correct, the answer is certainly positive because the history of Dún Ailinne spans a period that precedes the Roman conquest of Britain. Iron Age datable finds of the site are, in fact, attributable to a period covering the last centuries BC and terminating in the first century AD.[22] It would therefore have been impossible for Romans to be at the origin of Irish dairy farming since the process would have been established well in advance of the timing of their possible influence.

A few years later, Crabtree's interpretation was totally rejected by Finbar McCormick of Queen's University, Belfast. He strongly argued that 'the faunal evidence from Dún Ailinne suggests that dairying at this stage had not yet developed in Ireland'.[23]

The massive slaughtering of young calves at Dún Ailinne would be an unequivocal indication that cattle farming was primarily targeted at meat production since to fully exploit the food potential of each animal it is necessary to kill it while the balance between food and increase in body size is still economical.

This totally modifies the terms of the question. If cattle farming for milk was not a primary activity in Ireland in the period around the closing of the first and the opening of the second millennium but had become so prominent in Irish society in the sixth to seventh centuries AD, a profound change must have occurred in the meantime. The only way of explaining such a change is the Roman presence in Britain and the progressive introduction of dairy farming technologies from this country to Ireland. The Romans were masters in these technologies, particularly in the production of butter and cheese. The Irish word for cheese, *cáis*, is a clear derivation from the Latin *caseus*; butter-pats were *mescán* in Old Irish, similar to the Latin *mergo*, to plunge.[24]

These changes affected the quality of Irish life. If the efficiency of a water mill multiplied by 40 that of a traditional animal-operated mill, the production of dairy farming led to a five-fold increase in the amount of protein production using the same quantity of feed.[25]

In the Iron Age Ireland had been at a standstill.

The picture of Ireland left in the archeological record for the Iron Age is of a backward, impoverished island with dwindling agriculture, and a running down of Late Bronze Age technology, evidenced by miniaturisation and unmatched by a growing and thriving iron industry.[26]

A new Ireland now emerges that is no longer La Tène but not yet Christian. It is an Ireland into which Rome is slowly but decisively projecting its influence. It is the Roman Ireland that has been hidden or forgotten for so long.

The diffusion of new technologies, agricultural practice, social structures, and the appropriate settlement forms took place because the ideas were transferred from region to region by people, not necessarily by invasion or colonisation, but perhaps by traders and refugees, for example. It would seem, however, that the major influx of ideas, and perhaps some people, were reaching Ireland from Britain and Europe, not in the early Iron Age but in the Roman period, and that was the adoption or introduction of Roman-derived rather than La Tène iron technology and craft practices that brought about the agricultural expansion and social change resulting in pressure on land and in the adoption of the defended farmsteads in Ireland.[25]

RING FORTS AND THE NEW LANDSCAPE

It is now possible to start afresh. This new start is marked by an astonishing proliferation of ring forts. Thousands will dot the Irish landscape and witness the beginning of the Irish revival. Why this new appearance? What is their function? Were they imported or a native development? What is their dating? And, most importantly, what is their connection with the Roman world?

All these questions are closely interrelated and not easy to disentangle. We have seen how Roman agricultural and farming techniques had progressively permeated Ireland setting the scene for a major shift in social life. We also know that, despite their name, ring forts had no military scope but were, essentially, a new type of farmstead. It appears legitimate to come to the conclusion that ring forts were the response to the new agricultural upheaval and the introduction of dairy farming as a primary source of alimentation.

The connection is almost certainly there, but is the emergence of ring forts to be directly related to the introduction of Roman techniques, or were these just activating a new context in which ring forts eventually developed? To answer this we need to tackle the 'red herring' of the chronology of ring forts, in particular whether they belong to the first or second half of the first millennium.[28]

When excavated the earliest examples of ring forts were attributed to the sixth century AD. This starting date for ring forts has been subsequently stretched forward and backward to fill, on the one hand, the archaeological void of the Late Bronze Age and the Iron Age and to firmly establish these sites well into the medieval period, on the other hand. In both cases the risk of a direct Roman influence would be removed and ring forts could be seen as an indigenous development. Without embarking on such a controversial matter, it can be noted that no phenomenon of such importance and magnitude happens abruptly and that, while there is not enough ground at the moment for a major pre-dating, there is sufficient evidence supporting an earlier dating by a few centuries in time,[29] well into the period of direct Roman influence.

Substantial evidence supports this interpretation. In Britain several Roman and sub-Roman farmsteads similar to the Irish ring forts have been excavated, particularly in Wales and Scotland, that could be the origin of Irish ring forts. Against this reading it has been suggested that the development of enclosed farmsteads in areas of Britain close to Ireland could rather be 'the product of similar agricultural advances and a comparable social structure'.[30] However, it could also be linked to important changes in Romano-British military architecture. Such change did not occur in the north or in the west but on the south and east coasts. Here Roman forts which have had for centuries a square shape, went through a most remarkable transformation and developed circular shapes, dramatically different from the straight lines of previous periods. These forts were closely associated with the Roman fleet in Britain, some were only accessible by sea, and the fleet was an excellent vehicle for spreading,

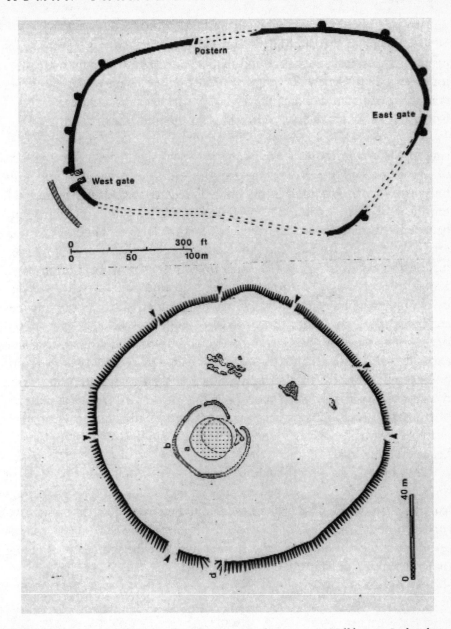

Figure 9. Saxon shore fort in Britain (top) and Freestone Hillfort in Ireland (bottom).

directly or indirectly, new habits around the North Sea.

The Romano-British, fourth-century Saxon shore fort at Pevensey, for instance, shows a distinctive round shape that resembles that of many Irish forts, such as the one at Freestone Hill, County Kilkenny. Here, together with a Roman coin dated c. AD 337-340, various artefacts were found of Roman or sub-Roman style that belong to the mid-fourth century AD.

This is not an isolated case. The presence of Roman material in Irish ring forts is not infrequent. Sometimes it is very significant. The ring forts of Garranes and Garryduff, among the oldest excavated, stand only miles from Cork Harbour, in the immediate rich agricultural hinterland, the ideal place to exploit the new Roman agricultural techniques and benefit by Roman influence from the sea. At Garranes the most important collection of Roman and sub-Roman pottery, more than 250 fragments, was found together with other objects of clear Roman inspiration: a superbly decorated button of bronze, back and edges tinned, a design in champlevé enamel on the face, trumpet and triskele motifs and red enamelling; together with three pieces of millefiori glass, a legacy from the Roman world.[31] In Garryduff, toilet implements similar to those excavated in Roman contexts were discovered together with shards of post-Roman pottery, an interlaced glass stud and three interlaced stone trial pieces. Irish interlacing most probably originated from the patterns of Romano-British mosaics. In Garryduff a sickle was also found which in the report of the excavation is related to a similar sickle found in the Leacanabuaile fort.[32]

We can thus see why the inhabitants of that fort changed the form of their houses from round to square. The change in shape appears the logical response on the part of the Leacanabuaile people to a different environment, new priorities and new needs. It also appears as another landmark in understanding how the Roman world contributed to changing the Irish landscape and the Irish way of life.

CHAPTER 4

Latin and the Origin of Literacy in Ireland

It took perhaps one million years from the moment an hominid started using language as a means of communication to the moment when, around 6,000 years ago, the first written inscriptions appeared, marking the beginning of great early civilisations. We conventionally call the first of these two periods prehistory and the second history. The beginning of history in Ireland coincides with the appearance of ogham inscriptions.

Similar to runes, ogham inscriptions are composed of a series of strokes with different orientation in respect of a vertical baseline, each stroke corresponding to a particular sound. More than 300 standing stones with ogham inscriptions have been found scattered in the southern countryside with special concentration in Counties Kerry, Cork and Waterford but also in Wales, Devon, Cornwall and the Isle of Man. Many ogham inscriptions have been displaced from their original context and, despite their first appearance, are not necessarily associated with a grave, their most probable use being that of memorials or cenotaphs. As with other early cultures, the appearance of literacy is not an exciting matter. In Ireland most ogham just confine themselves to the name of the person commemorated, sometimes accompanied by the patronymic or the gentile name. In a number of cases this name is a Latin one: Amadus from *Amatus*, Mariani from *Marianus*, Marin from *Marinus*, Sagittari from *Sagittarius*, Vitalin from *Vitalinus*, Colomagni from *Columba*.

FROM PAGAN TO THE LAST TO CHRISTIAN TO THE FIRST
Do these names indicate a foreign origin or connection of ogham

inscriptions? The very question was at first rejected as an absurdity. The inscriptions, it has been argued, were an entirely native practice originated in the pagan, Celtic Ireland of druids, legends and encrypted codes of communication. In 1879 an attempt was even made to force obvious Latin names, such as Marianus and Sagittarius, into the most incredible reading of 'the field of Ryan' and 'the sage/priest Dari' respectively.[1]

This was at the time of strong patriotic feelings and the idea that the Roman empire should have direct or indirect influence on the shaping of Irish culture, was not very welcome. Even more so since it was increasingly evident that such influence had been largely mediated by the Romano-British culture, thus making Britain again the centre of crucial developments in Irish history.

Perhaps no one more than Eoin MacNeill symbolises this approach. Co-founder of the Gaelic League and later president of the Irish volunteers, he was a statesman and a scholar at the same time. MacNeill studied ogham inscriptions and even produced, in 1909 and 1931, two articles on this subject in the *Proceedings of the Royal Irish Academy*. He strongly rejected any Christian origin for ogham inscriptions (another way of contaminating the roots of Irish Celtic culture with spurious, external factors) as well as any relationship between Ireland and Imperial Rome.

In his view ogham was 'pagan to the last' and ogham inscriptions had to be seen as the druidic response to the cultural dominion of Rome, a reaction to the imposition of Latin as the universal language of the empire. As late as 1945, R.A.S. Macalister, the author of *Corpus Inscritionum Insularum Celticarum*, an authority in the field, reiterated the primitive, secret character of ogham inscriptions.

The tide was, however, changing and in a drastic way. The pagan theory was unable to explain why most of the ogham inscriptions belong to the fifth and sixth century, as linguistic analysis was progressively but surely showing to be the case. If this was the dating, then the answer was a logical one: ogham inscriptions were essentially Christian inscriptions. Damian McManus, an expert in this area, seems to be convinced that this is the case:

There is nothing in the nature of an ogham memorial which precludes the possibility that the subject of its inscription was a Christian ... and the cult of inscribing ogham memorials flourished during the early Christian era.[2]

The fact that these are not pagan inscriptions and that nothing precludes them from being Christian does not, however, close the matter. Nobody would argue that a number of oghams certainly commemorate Christians and that several bear an engraved cross, the very symbol of Christianity. The point is that most, if not all, such crosses were added later on pre-existing ogham inscriptions. As V.E. Nash-Williams, a fundamental reference for Dark Age archaeology, points out:

The use of the cross as a Christian symbol was a comparatively late development. St Paul glories in the cross as the symbol of Christ's Passion, but the first Christians in general shrunk from identifying Christianity with the pagan instrument of capital punishment. Crucifixion was abolished by Constantine, but the old repugnance to the use of the symbol persisted through the fourth century, and it was only in the fifth that the cross in its true shape began to come into general use. The only certain occurrence of the cross in Wales at this time is on a late monument coming perhaps at the very end of the series. Crosses found on certain of the other stones are, probably later additions, representing re-use of the stones in the succeeding phase.[3]

This is certainly the case for the stone of Dobitucus, standing in the churchyard in the village of Clydai in Pembrokeshire, South Wales. We do not know who Dobitucus was, nor do we know exactly when the stone was first erected. But we know that at some time, from two to four centuries later according to Nash-Williams, the stone was reset in the ground head downwards and then, but only then, a ring-cross was carved in it. The important thing is that the ring-cross obliterates the last letters of the Latin inscription, an unequivocal sign that the cross was a later addition to the inscription. So it is for the vast majority of cases: Christianity was taking possession of pre-existing monuments, not just creating them.

Figure 10. The stone of Dobitucus.

Clamped between the alternatives of Pagan/Christian, Irish scholars were misled in their search for an explanation of the origins of ogham inscriptions. The simple fact to be recognised was that Rome could have played a role in such origins, independently and before the arrival of Christianity in Ireland. It has taken a long time but at last such a recognition is taking pace. Most of the arguments have always been at hand, it was only a matter of looking at them with new eyes and addressing the question with a fresh mind.

LATIN AND OGHAM INSCRIPTIONS

No doubt ogham is a cypher of the Latin alphabet. The twenty characters of ogham correspond to the letters of that alphabet. It required, therefore, a basic knowledge of the phonetical significance of those characters in Latin and the ability to structure them into a new alphabetical system. It required, in fact, much more: the full understanding of the grammatical classification of such characters within the Latin language.

The starting model was most probably that of the most famous Latin grammarian of all times, Aelius Donatus, whose name has remained for centuries synonymous with grammar for millions of students up to very recent times. In his *Ars Maior*, produced around the middle of the fourth century AD, he proposes his classification of the letters of the Latin alphabet, as shown in the first table. What happened next is most uncertain but the logic seems clear when you study the second table. Five of the mutes (in bold) were used to form a group in the ogham alphabet. Five of the semi-vowels (in bold) contributed to another group. The vowels remained untouched and formed another group yet. X, K, P and Y were eliminated as unnecessary and superfluous. A final group was constituted of all residual characters to whom NG was added. The final result is shown in the third table.

Latin, including its grammatical intricacies, was then well known to the people who introduced ogham inscriptions in Ireland. But also the spelling system of such inscriptions is based on Latin usage. The key to this argument is in the recurrent use of double symbols on ogham stones.

A mile and a half from Dingle, on the Dingle peninsula, nine ogham

DONATUS CLASSIFICATION								
vocales – vowels	A	E	I	O	U			
semivocales – semi-vowels	F	L	M	N	R	S	X	
mutae – mutes	B	C	D	G	H	K	P	Q	T
Graecae litterae – Greek letters	Y	Z						

TRANSFORMATIONS								
vocales – vowels	A	E	I	O	U			
semivocales – semi-vowels	F/V	L	M/B	N	R	S	[X]	
mutae – mutes	B	C	D	G	H	[K]	[P]	Q	T
Graecae litterae – Greek letters	[Y]	Z						

OGHAM				
group one – vowels	A	E	I	O	U
group two – semi-vowels	N	S	F	L	B
group three – mutes	Q	C	T	D	H
group four – residual	R	Z	**NG**	G	M

stones lie on the ground of an ancient circular enclosure. They bear crosses and, most important for our purpose, duplication of several consonants in the inscription. In *Early Ireland, A Field Guide,* it is suggested that duplication may have occurred because the cutters were paid at piece-rates and those who commissioned them were not able to read ogham.[4]

In reality duplication was essentially a matter of pronunciation closely linked to the evolution of the Irish language, with scholars still engaged in lively discussions on this controversial issue. What it is important to note here is that Latin accepts the use of double consonants internally but not at the beginning of a word and that Irish closely follows this Latin rule. It means that Irish on ogham stones was spelt in line with Latin orthographic conventions.

> ... what it shows is that the ogham orthography used in the inscriptions does not accurately match the sound-pattern of the Irish language being represented. What it does much, very much better, is the sound-pattern of classical Latin. The people who set up the ogham stones must therefore have been quite familiar with, and influenced by, the Latin language as written in the Roman alphabet. Very likely they could even write it themselves ...[5]

Latin was, therefore, unequivocally at the origin of the ogham alphabet. At this point two questions remain to be answered: when and how ogham was introduced in Ireland?

THE DICE OF BALLINDERRY

Dating is always difficult for stone monuments, like oghams, which are in most cases out of context and to which radiocarbon dating and dendrochronology cannot be applied. We have, however, a starting and a closing date for their invention: not *before* the first century BC, when the letter Z was introduced into Latin as the last letter of the alphabet, and not *later* than the fourth century AD when the grammarian Donatus wrote his *Ars Maior*. Within this period everything is possible and the trend has been in recent years towards an earlier date for the origin of ogham inscriptions. Donatus, it is argued, did not invent the categorisation linked to his name that substantially draws from the work of earlier writers, most notably the second-century Varro.[6]

Even earlier than that, Quintilian, writing about AD 95, refers to the method used to teach Roman children the alphabet, a method that clearly anticipates the Donatus classification.[7] A dating of the second or third century AD has been proposed and seems to attract growing consensus.[8]

In Ballinderry, County Offaly, during the excavations carried out in

1942, a bone dice was unearthed which seems to provide the key to the dating of ogham inscriptions. Three of its six sides are marked with dots corresponding to the numbers three, four and six. Number one and number two are not marked since they would be on the end parts of the bone. Number five is marked but not with five dots. What we find, instead, is the ogham letter F/V, the exact equivalent of the Roman numeral V, for five. The person who made the dice was certainly familiar not only with the Roman alphabet but also with Roman numerals and, most importantly, would use elements of both the Irish and Roman languages in a complementary way as part of an integrated, rather than distinct and separated cultural background. The dice, dating most likely from the second century AD, confirms the assumptions made above and puts the origin of ogham firmly into the classical Roman period.

By moving from the elegant abstractions of linguistics into the archaeological and historical reality of the second and third century AD, we can finally appreciate the full significance and fundamental importance of ogham in the shaping of Irish culture. We know by now that a progressive process of Romanisation was underway in the entire empire and that Ireland was not immune from this process. We know that Latin was the *lingua franca* of the empire and that literacy was more widespread than has long been believed. It is quite natural to suppose that the process of Romanisation of Ireland was accompanied by the progressive penetration not only of Roman or Romano-inspired objects, techniques and ways of life but also of Latin.

Ogham inscriptions not only confirm this process, but introduce revolutionary elements into the picture. If originating in the second-third century, as it is now largely assumed, they would bear witness to the opening of Ireland to literacy through direct classical Roman influence at a time when no other European country wrote in the vernacular. If writing is the beginning of history, at that moment, well before the arrival of Christianity, the roots of Irish history are definitely established.

This is a native, conceivably pre-Christian tradition of literacy, possibly, though not necessarily, extremely limited in scope, but which nonetheless leaves traces of its existence both on ogham stones and in some of the earliest surviving writing from Ireland, distinguishable from the orthographic system of Old and Middle Irish which is well known to owe much to the educational efforts of fifth- and sixth-century Christian missionaries from sub-Roman Britain.

All this substantiates the proposition that the ogham stones are the surviving evidence of a well-established writing system, far less limited than the limited inscriptions on stone suggest at a first glance. If ogham orthography had not been well established in the ordinary uses of literacy in Ireland there would have been no contest with the Britannic system that came in with St Patrick and his successors.[9]

THE INDO-EUROPEAN CONNECTION

It had all started long before the arrival of a form of writing, originating in Latin, in Ireland; well before ogham inscriptions, in a geographical area that nobody has yet been able to identify with certainty; with the appearance of a language, Indo-European, considered the ancestral cradle of so many modern languages. The fact that the word horse is *asva-s* in Sanskrit, *aspa* in Persian, *Eppo* in Gaulish, *ippos* in Greek, *Ecco* in Illyrian, *equus* in Latin, *ebol* in Welsh and *ech* in Irish, cannot be by chance – as it is not by chance that *ewe* in English is parallelled by *oi* in old Irish, *ois* in Greek and *ovis* in Latin. Common lexical sources must have been at their origin, and the more the similarities, the more the affinities between the different languages.

There is an important range of words with a common heritage, cognate words as the linguists like to call them, to be found in Latin and Irish that would appear to have a shared Indo-European matrix. It is possible that such cognate words were the result of early regional contacts among Indo-European speaking populations, which could have been at the origin of both Italic and Celtic languages.

These and other factors could suggest an earlier geographical continuity between the ancestors of Italic and Celtic speakers. If so, there is, I fear, no means whereby we can say where this region was situated, how large it was or when various groups found themselves dwelling in it or passing through it. There are no grounds for postulating primeval cultural and linguistic conglomerate of people from which Celts and Italics split off, the former to populate Central Europe, France, Spain, Britain and Ireland; the latter to settle in the peninsula of Italy. On the other hand, it is feasible to suppose that groups of people spoke varieties of Indo European which became more closely related through neighbourhood and contact: that these people lived to the north of the Alps, and that speakers of Italic and Celtic ultimately derived their languages from them. There would seem to be nothing primarily objectionable about agreeing with Dillon that the various peoples might have begun to make their moves in the latter part of the second millennium BC.[10]

Cognate words span a variety of areas and topics. In the fundamental area of agriculture and farming we have already noted the close lexical relations between the words for horse and sheep in Latin and Irish. Close relations also exist between the words for bull, *tarbh* and *taurus* in Irish and Latin respectively, (pig) *orc* and *porcus,* (lamb) *uan* and *agnus.* As far as these basic animals are concerned there does not seem to be a problem with a common origin, but when we enter the area of plants, agriculture, stock breeding and techniques where, as we have seen the influence of Rome has been a major one, the distinction between cognate and loan words (those borrowed from one language to another) is not so simple. The frequently invoked criterion that a number of such words are a clear reflection of an original Indo-European pastoral-agricultural culture and should therefore be considered cognate rather than loan-words, can work to a certain point since the Latin/Roman culture embodies most of such 'typical' features and naturally so for its Indo-European origin. The existence of close similarities between an Irish word and those in a significant number of other Indo-European languages usually facilitates the choice. There are, however, cases where this choice is not so straightforward.

We find, for instance , close similarities between the words for honey *(mil) mel,* snake, in the two forms of *nahir (natrix)* and *(escung) anguis,* and silver *(argat) argentum,* in Irish and Latin respectively, all with cognates in other Indo-European languages. However, tradition has it that snakes never inhabited the island, bee-keeping seems to have been introduced to Ireland by early monks and silver first appeared in Ireland only as a consequence of contacts with the Roman world in the early centuries AD. Why the Irish had these words in their original vocabulary, if they really had them, and why they are so closely related to Latin, remains a linguistic mystery, despite all attempts at an explanation.

Other cognate or pseudo-cognate words can be assembled into three major groups referring to three major areas of life and contact:

– family, kinship, social organisation. and daily life

king	-	ri-rex
brother	-	bráthair-frater
man	-	fear-vir
old	-	sean-senex
sister	-	siúr-soror
dog	-	cú-canis
eat	-	ithe-edere
language	-	teanga-lingua
peace	-	siothcháin-situs (rest, inactivity)

– commerce, transport and the military

boat	-	nau-navis
wheel	-	roth-rota
axle	-	ais-axis
wagon	-	car-currus
shield	-	shiath-scutum

– environment and nature

land	-	tír-terra
sea	-	muir-mare
river	-	abhainn-amnis
to mow	-	meitheal (group of reapers)-metere
willow	-	sail-salix
fish	-	íasc-piscis
water	-	uisce-unda

This is an important linguistic background and one that needs to be handled with care. While, for instance, the word *iasc* for fish in Irish is a true cognate, the Indo-European word was lost in Breton and had to be borrowed later from the Latin world. Perhaps it only survived in the name of the river Usk (Wysg). Or does Usk derive from *uisce* (water) as the word whiskey (water of life) does? Distinguishing between cognate and loan-words is not a simple matter and it is even more difficult, perhaps, distinguishing between early and later loan words.

EARLY LATIN LOAN-WORDS

Almost 600 Roman words were borrowed by the Celts and about 160 Celtic words by the Romans. They eventually came to cover almost all aspects of culture from war to trade, from domestic life to food, from building to religion. How many Roman words were borrowed by the Irish we do not exactly know because many of the early borrowings may have been replaced by later equivalents, but certainly a number of them made their entry into Ireland in very early times, perhaps as early as the third century AD.[11]

Among early borrowings a selected number of words of a secular nature can be identified which would bear witness to pre-Patrician linguistic contacts between the Roman empire and Ireland, particularly in the areas of trade and the military. As we have seen, these are areas that were key contacts between the Celtic and the Roman world since very early times. It comes, therefore, as no surprise that such words were also introduced to Ireland very early.

The list of words that were appropriated is significant in this respect. In addition to *corcra, purpura,* purple dye, primarily used by members of the Irish upper class, it includes *cróch, crocus,* saffron dye, a traditional Irish dye very popular, together with black, with the lower classes, to the point that *cróch* is often referred to as a native dye. However, once we know that it derives from the Latin *crocus,* it must be said that *crocus* was one of the favourite colours of Greek and Roman ladies, as can still be seen in the pictures discovered at Herculaneum and Pompei. Dresses of this colour were commonly called *vestae crocata* in Latin, and a special corporation of *crocotarii* specialised in Rome in the dying of what, many centuries later would be called saffron from the Arab *za'fran*, yellow. The Irish themselves used the word *cróch* to indicate the colour yellow in general and made recourse to a great variety of different dyestuffs to produce this colour. The plant *crocus sativus, cróch an fhómhair*, was apparently introduced in Ireland only in early AD 1000.

Gold (*ór, aurum*) and wine (*fíon, vinum*) but also *esarn, exhibernum* (year-old wine), that were so much liked and traded by Celts, are on this list. The National Museum of Ireland keeps about 600 ounces of gold in its collections, more than all other European museums, with the only exception of Athens. Such quantities of gold could not originate only from the alluvial gold of County Wicklow.

The list continues with *séu, sextarius*, the sixth part of *congius*, a Roman measure of liquid capacity, equivalent to three and a quarter litres. Divided by six it is almost exactly the equivalent of a pint. This needs to be seen in connection with *muidhe, modius; creiter, cratera; canna, panna;* and *síothal, situla*, a series of Roman containers and vessels for multiple purposes, but essentially for liquids, that entered Irish life at a very early stage together with the word and use of another container *ces, cista*, a basket.

The list also includes *piobar, piper*, pepper. Well known to the Romans both for its medical and preservative capacities, it was imported from as far away as India and Java, crossing almost the entire Roman empire to reach Britain and eventually Ireland. Further in the list, the word *ingor, ancora* (anchor recalls very early contacts by sea with Latin-speaking people). Among the first words likely to be used on these occasions *monad, moneta*, money and *díorna, denarius*, a type of Roman coin used in Irish in the broader sense of weight, are also on the list.

The name of the Roman god *Mercurius* in the Irish form *Mercúir* is an early borrowing too. Mercury is the most popular Roman divinity in Britain, often represented as a trader god loaded with a wide variety of Celtic connotations. Finally, Irish words like *arm, legio* and *trebun* witness early military contacts with the Roman world, including the presence of Irish troops in the Roman army.

The scenario that emerges from these words is certainly not that of an exclusively Celtic or of a Christian Ireland. It is, instead, one of a country having close contacts with and knowledge of the Roman empire.[12]

LITERACY BEFORE CHRISTIANITY

This is a scenario that has been for long rejected and the importance of which has only been recently understood and valued both in archaeological and in linguistic terms. A counter-scenario had been set up, once again, by MacNeill who, in his 1931 *Beginning of Latin culture in Ireland*, introduced an interpretation of the way in which Latin loan-words had made their way into Irish which was to last for decades and, still today, die very hard in the general belief. This interpretation was based on two main assumptions: firstly that, apart from minor intrusions, Latin loan-words were introduced into Irish by Christianity; and secondly that this happened at given moments in time, in the fifth century, in correspondence with the evangelisation of Saint Patrick and his disciples, or later in the sixth century in connection with the monastic development. These two waves of borrowing would be reflected in the different Irish versions of *Cothriche* and *Padrig* for the Latin word *Patricius,* Patrick. The *Two Patricks* even become the title of a book by T.F. O'Rahilly, ten years later, suggesting that the borrowing of the Latin loan-words occurred, instead, essentially in the fifth century and that the different versions of the word Patrick were due to different pronunciation by different groups of missionaries there who introduced words in Ireland.

All this is now strongly challenged by a new school of linguists. The fact that literacy could be exclusively linked to Christianisation appears increasingly improbable. Not only because of ogham inscriptions and of examples of very early borrowings, but because the impressive development of Latin associated with Christianisation would have simply been impossible without some pre-existing familiarity with Latin. The conclusion that the introduction of Latin, as an essential aspect of the Romanisation of Ireland, preceded Christianisation is now shared, although with different emphasis and argument, by some of the best scholars. According to J. Stevenson:

The assumption that non-Christian academic Irishmen of the fourth and fifth centuries, before the arrival of St Patrick, did not write in Irish script (or perhaps in Latin) is invalid, based on the permanence of ogham as used for memorial inscriptions, together with a set of unexamined assumptions about the nature of Roman culture and the general premise that no-one in Europe wrote in the vernacular so early, which is, on the Gaulish evidence alone, unacceptable.[13]

For A. Harvey:

> As for the Latin language ... I hope I have made it clear why I believe we must reckon with that as a potent force in the cultural life not only of Britain, but also of Ireland, about and indeed well before the year AD 500.[14]

In the view of D. Ó Cróinín:

> The flowering of literature and learning in early Ireland is indelibly linked with the rise of Christian monastic schools, which come to prominence from the second half of the sixth century. But the Latin script used in Ireland is clearly a much older development, and it will be worth our while trying to trace the origins of that script and the beginning of literacy in Ireland.[15]

As to the assumption that the borrowing of Latin loan words happened at given moments in time, this is also progressively abandoned because of its static and fragmented vision of a phenomenon, that of the increasing interchange between the Roman and the Irish cultures, which was instead an articulated and dynamic one. Rather than linguistic waves linked to waves of Christianisation, the entry of Latin loan-words into the Irish language was a continuum that started in the very early centuries of the first millennium and developed in the following centuries with increasing intensity, marking the introduction of literacy in Ireland.

Within this continuous flow it is difficult to establish temporal sequences but some general chronological development can be identified. We have already seen how the beginning of ogham inscriptions could be dated back to the second century AD and that early Latin loan-words could have been borrowed as early as the third century. The borrowing following that, in the middle of the fifth century, was most likely that of words which were introduced into the Irish language at a time when the Irish could not pronounce the letter P, and which was consequently changed into C. To this group belongs the word purple, Latin *purpura, corcra* in Irish, but also words like plant, *planta* in Latin, *cland* in Irish; feather, *pluma, clúmh*; fist, *cuan, pugnus;* mantel, *pallium, caille;* and easter, *pascha, cásc.*

From the mid-fifth to the mid-sixth centuries, a series of crucial modifications occur in the Irish language such as lenition, the weakening of certain consonants, apocope, the loss of final syllables in the word, or syncope, the loss of internal syllables. Depending on the presence or not of such changes it may be determined when a Roman loan-word was introduced into Irish. On this basis we can, for instance, say that words like abbot, *abbaith, abbatem;* baptism, *baptisma, baiste;* veal, *vitulum fithal;* sin, *peccatum, peccath;* cross, *crucem, croch;* physician, *medicus, mindech,* where lenition is present, cannot be dated before AD 450. Lenition also meant that a number of Latin words starting with F had their initial changed into S and can also be dated at about this point in time. These include bean, *faba, seib;* window, *fenestra, senester;* fibula, *fibula, sibal;* oven, *furnus, sorn;* and flake, *flosccus, sloch.* Similarly, for words like February, *Februarius, Feabra;* oil, *oleum, olae;* martyrdom, *martirium, martrae;* notar, *notarius, notaire,* where apocope is present, the earliest dating can be put at around AD 500.

Syncope and syncopated loan-words appeared in the middle of the sixth century and determined not only a further reduction in the length of words but also, as a consequence, the re-introduction in Irish of previously lost groups of consonants such as *nt.* On this basis we can say, for instance, that the word penance, *pennaind* in Irish, borrowed from the Latin *pententia,* pre-dates AD 550 because the cluster *nt* in Latin was substituted by the cluster *nd* in Irish, thus showing that syncope had not yet occurred when borrowing took place. Instead, in the case of words such as people, *gentil, gentes;* intention, *intinn, intentio;* or contention, *contan, contentio,* the cluster *nt* appears and the borrowing can be dated after AD 550. In the meantime, Latin loan-words starting with P were progressively introduced into Irish without the need of changing P into C. Some of these words were perhaps introduced much earlier than usually believed, already in the middle of the fifth century, but substantial borrowing occurred in the fifth century, to become a real linguistic wave from AD 550 onwards.

When in the sixth and seventh centuries AD the very first examples of manuscripts appear in Irish, Latin had fully made its way into Irish and had been an integral part in the long process that accompanied the passage of Irish from oral communication to literacy. By that time Latin had also become the language of the learned man and the sons of the ruling élite. Future monks were introduced to both Latin and Irish in the monastic schools, a symbiosis that was to develop up to the twelfth century. For the ordinary Irish, however, all this had very little bearing, except perhaps when listening, without great understanding, to the mass in Latin on holy days. But the same Irish would speak a language with hundreds of words borrowed from Latin and would, in their daily lives, refer to place names which had a Latin origin or root. Those who would be able to write would use Latin letters and some would have, when dead, their names inscribed on a stone, using ogham inscriptions originating from the Roman alphabet. They would probably be largely unaware of all this as they would be unaware that the introduction of literacy in Ireland had been the result of a long process, which started well before the arrival of Christianity, when Latin was still the language of the Roman empire.

CHAPTER 5

A Second Invasion?

DIGGING INTO THE ROCK OF CASHEL

It is the name of more than 50 ancient stone forts, villages and towns of Ireland, and it is part of the name of 50 more. The word is cashel, the anglicised version of the Irish *caiseal,* straight from the Latin *castellum*, a small *castrum*, to indicate a castle or a fortress. The plural of *castrum (castra)* indicates, however, something different, a military camp or fortification, and is still incorporated in the name Chester and in those of many other English towns which originated from such Roman camps.

Among the many cashels, Cashel in Tipperary is the most famous, a special place loaded with history and legends. Here St Patrick accidentally stabbed his crozier into the foot of the local king, Corc, or possibly his brother Oenghus, and the poor victim, believing this to be part of some new exotic rite of initiation, bore the pain without a word.

Why not prefer to borrow from the English *castle* or, better still, from an Irish derivation of *cíos-ail*, rent rock, referring to the fact that Cashel was once the capital city of Munster and that here its kings received their rents? A mere fancy, according to the best scholars. The English word *castle* derives also from the Latin *castellum* and while there are cases of names in Ireland which indicate the corruption of *cashel* into castle (the case of Ballycastle, *Baile an-chaisil,* County Mayo, or Casteldargan, *Caiseal Locha-Deargain,* County Sligo) there is no indication of cases the other way around. As to the Irish origin this is clearly contradicted by the fact that there are so many cashels in Ireland to which the explanation given for the rock in Tipperary would not apply.[1]

While the origin of the word cashel is undoubtedly in the Latin *castellum*, it only became associated with many places in Ireland in later medieval times. Why should the same argument not be valid for Cashel in Tipperary? Apart from fascinating but largely unconfirmed stories, the oldest certain evidence there is the building of Cormac's Chapel in 1127. Adventuring into retrospective interpretations would have been a vain exercise until very recently.

Until 1992 excavations were made in Cormac's Chapel for the first time and it became possible to dig into the early history of the Rock of Cashel. What was found were not the graves of the kings of Munster nor St Patrick's crozier but skeletons of ordinary people, together with several sherds of imported pottery. Many are amphorae of Mediterranean origin dating from around the mid-sixth century, which opens a completely new archaeological horizon. But two conjoining sherds, found in the earlier occupation layer, close to where the excavators met the stone of the rock, have an even more interesting profile. Decorated with two horizontal grooves and wheel burnished, the sherds are made of hard mid-gray fabric with occasional sand and some fine rounded ironstone, a completely different composition from the Mediterranean ones. A composition like this could indicate a Merovingian or Carolingian provenance as well as a Romano-British one: it takes an expert eye to recognise the difference, the eye of Dr Jerry Evans, to whom the sherds were sent for identification. He found that the fabric of the sherds is much finer and better manufactured than that of Merovingian or Carolingian objects and most probably of Romano-British origin.[2] If so the two sherds could pre-date the Mediterranean ware and move the origin of Cashel back in time to the fourth or fifth century AD. Starting from this, the history of Cashel should perhaps be entirely rewritten.

The rewriting would involve the possibility of a fourth-century military expedition in the area, leading to the establishment of a military camp or fort in Cashel itself. Not a fort of the traditional Roman type in regular, rectangular shape, but the new type of fortress in more irregular, roundish shape which was usual in the last part of the fourth century, particularly on the south-west coasts of Britain, the so-called Saxon

Shore. We have already seen how the shape of ring forts in Ireland could have originated from this new type of Roman fort. In a more direct way, this could also be the case with Cashel, the shape of whose enclosure reveals similarities with that of Roman military installations of that period.

The idea of a second Roman expedition in the Tipperary area has for long tantalised the specialists:

> Can we really escape the conclusion that at least the aristocracy of the south-west were Romanised Britons and Gauls , and is there even reason to suspect a military campaign in the area?[3]

> Another suggestion, even more intriguing, has sometimes been mooted ... has caused some historians to wonder whether we have archaeological evidence for an abortive military intrusion which came to grief in County Tipperary.[4]

Proving this idea is another matter. It requires answering the same fundamental questions raised in respect of the first invasion: why, when, by whom, how and under what circumstances? But now we have no historian, like Tacitus, to help us set the scene. We must rely exclusively on archaeological evidence, and since the assumption is that a second invasion reached Tipperary, we will start by looking around there to find the possible signs of such an invasion.

A ROMAN SOLDIER IN THE TIPPERARY AREA?

A few miles west of Tipperary, in the townland of Balline near the village of Knocklong, James Flynn was digging in 1940 for gravel when he discovered a silver hoard, one of the most important finds of Roman material in Ireland. The Balline hoard, as it became known, consists of seven pieces: two silver ingots, parts of two others, and three fragments of silver dishes, all attributable to the fourth century AD.

One fragment is the beaded rim of a dish, the second is from the corner of another dish ornamented with leaves, quatrefoils and acanthus patterns, the third is probably from the flat bottom of a third dish show-ing part of a hunting scene with three horsemen. The three pieces are in the purest Romano-British tradition of the late empire. The ingots are also typically Romano-British, of the type described as double-axe shaped, and belong to the same period. Three of the four ingots are inscribed with the name of the officials responsible for attesting the quan-tity and quality of the metal contained therein. One inscription, *Ex Officina Isatis,* is exactly the same as that of an ingot found in the Roman fort of Richborough, and it even appears that the two inscriptions were made with the same stamp.

These are the visible features, but the two complete ingots have another feature which is of special interest to us: their weight, 317g and 318g respectively, are almost exactly the weight of a Roman pound. Such an apparently minor detail hardly fits into the traditional picture of hoards being nothing but loot from Irish raiders plundering an agonised Roman empire. If we are not talking of randomly looted pieces of pre-cious metal but of a precise, officially standardised amount of silver, this is a different picture, the ingots having their own specific function and lit-tle or nothing to do with looting.

Indeed, the very presumption that hoards indicate looting is under severe strain. Certainly Irish raids multiplied towards the end of the empire, but it is most likely that the Irish had been plundering the British coasts, though with less success, well before this period with Roman sub-jects doing the same in the other direction when the opportunity arose. This was normal practice in those days and the idea of Irish raiders as predecessors of modern pirates is nothing but a romantic fable.

If looting was the rule rather than the exception and if hoards were linked to looting, we should then see, all along, a clear parallel between the number of hoards buried in Britain by people wanting to protect their valuables, and hoards discovered in Ireland, as well as some consistent pattern between the intensity of raids and the frequency of such hoards. This is not the case.

It used to be thought, for instance, that the concentration of later third-century coin hoards around the coasts of south Wales was related

to increased attacks by Irish raiders, a guess that has been now abandoned since there are no equivalent hoards of Roman booty from Irish
sites from that period.[5] It is also now clear that, despite the increase in
raids in the fourth and fifth century there was not a major increase in the
number of hoards in Britain compared to previous centuries:

> There is a natural tendency to seek in gold and silver hoards of the later
> fourth century evidence for the impending collapse of the Roman adminis-
> tration in Britain, a collapse precipitated by events abroad but signalled by
> an apparent failure to prevent seaborne raiders attacking the island at will.
> Clearly such attacks will have produced a response in hoards although there
> is no special significant evidence for hoarding at the time of the great inva-
> sion by a combination of barbarian enemies in AD 367 ... It would appear
> in general that those with large sums of money to protect sought other
> means than hoarding and that panic-stricken hoarding does not characterise
> the last years of Roman Britain.[6]

Based on this evidence it is increasingly accepted that hoards were
accumulated and buried for many different reasons, looting being one of
them but certainly not the only, nor perhaps the most important one.
Hoards could be gathered as votive offerings, reserves of valuables, for
melting purposes by foundrymen (they often consisted of scrap material,
unfinished objects and ingots) or by merchants burying them at strategic
locations along their itinerary. The correlation between hoards and major
changes in the currency system is also very strong with peaks of hoards
occurring when the abrupt devaluation of the previous currency led to
lack of interest in and abandonment of such hoards. Finally, hoards can
be associated with military activities, and can constitute ransom money
to stop raiders' incursions and payment for military services. The presence and the characteristics of the ingots in the Balline hoard strongly
points to the last option. Could it be that the ingots were just part of the
stipendium paid to a soldier in the Roman army, perhaps an Irish feder-
ate who campaigned under Roman banners in the Tipperary area?

It could. Contacts with the Roman army must have been more than

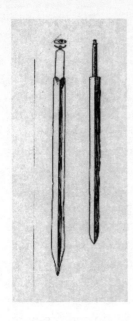

Irish La Tène swords from Lagore (left).

Roman Gladius and Spatha from Newstead (right).

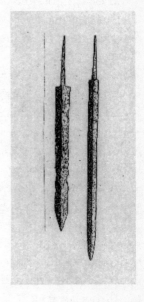

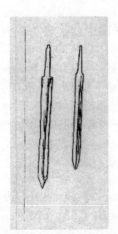

Early Christian Irish swords from Lagore (left).

Figure 11. La Tène, Roman and Early Christian swords.

occasional, as shown by the Romanisation of some key features of Irish weaponry, in particular swords that underwent dramatic changes. Irish swords were leaf-shaped, triangular or parallel-sided, often with a strongly marked midrib and a curved bronze guard at their top. Under Roman influence they became much like the *spatha* or the *gladius*, characterised by square shoulders, a central ridge, parallel edges and a V-shaped point, though proportions may be noticeably different. The end of this process of assimilation is exemplified by some of the finds of early Christian swords in Lagore.

It is also possible that Irish *foederati* were serving in the Roman army. The answer is to be found in the occasional appearance of *Scotus, Scotius,* and in some cases *Hibernus,* in Latin inscriptions on the Continent, and even more so in the Latinised names of some ogham stones. The word *Sagittari* appears in an ogham inscription found at Burnfort, County Cork. What was a person named after the Latin word for archer doing there? And what was a *Galeatos,* in Latin someone wearing an helmet, a piece of equipment unknown in Ireland, doing in Killorglin, County Kerry? What indeed was CVNORIX MACVSMA QVICOLINE, the equivalent of Conri maac Maic-euillin in old Irish, doing within the defences of the Roman town at Exeter where an ogham stone still remembers him?[7]

If the Irish were serving in the Roman army it is most likely that they were involved in a second invasion of Ireland. The ingots of the Balline hoard could then be in payment for the services of one of them, and this is perfectly in line with imperial practice in those days. When acceding the throne in AD 361, Julian made a donation of five gold *solidi* and a pound of silver, exactly the same amount as the Balline ingots, to his soldiers. The Tipperary hypothesis begins to take shape.

... AND A ROMAN MILITARY EYE DOCTOR

We turn now eastwards to Golden, County Tipperary, to find another piece of the puzzle, a very singular and rare object; hardly 300 examples in the entire empire, only 30 in Britain, just one in Ireland. It is an oculist stamp, used by Roman doctors or healers to mark solid sticks of eye ointments, *collyria,* intended for subsequent infusion or dilution before application. How did an object like this find its way to Tipperary, and in the path of a Roman invading force? Let us start from the beginning.

The stamp was first described, one century and a half ago, in the *Archaeological Journal:*

> The tablet was discovered about the year 1842, in a dike on the rising ground above the green of the village of Golden Bridge, in a plot of land four acres in extent, known by the name of 'the Spittle Fields or Lands'. On this may yet be seen some ruins known traditionally as the hospital or infirmary. In the dike where the tablet was found a quantity of human bones have been brought to light. The singular object is very smooth, apparently formed of a piece of hardened fine-grained slate, of a dark green or blue colour, easily scratched with a knife, and the colour then appears of a light grey hue. Golden Bridge is on the river Suire, about a mile above the celebrated abbey of Athassel, founded AD 1200 by William de Burgo. At Golden there existed, in 1842, a remarkable circular castle which defended the bridge, but it has since fallen. It is possible to suppose that this stamp had been used in medieval times by some cunning leech who practised the healing art at the Spittle of Golden?[8]

The association of the stamp with human remains and the existence of a fort on an evidently important point of passage of the river Suir are highly suggestive of the possibility of a military connection, as the ruins of a hospital or infirmary are suggestive, perhaps too suggestive, of related medical activities. Only suggestions, maybe, but it is from these that the hypothesis of the stamp belonging to an oculist who followed the Roman *foederati* during a second invasion of Ireland towards the end of the fourth century started taking shape. Though dating is quite possible (oculist stamps of this period have been found in Britain), the hypothesis is quite controversial.

The stamp itself throws little light on the issue. A 36 x 36 x 7mm brick of green steatite, it bears the inscription: *M(ARCI) IUVENT(I) DIAMYSUS AD VET(ERE) CIC(ATRICES) or,* Marcus Iuventus

Tutianus' salve made from misy [probably copper pyrites] for old scars. Who Marcus Juventus Tutianus was we do not know. He could have been anyone in the medical profession (an itinerant doctor or a military doctor) and anyone, it has been argued, could have used the stamp, even a person totally divorced from the practice of medicine attracted by the fascination of the colour and the inscription, and perhaps its supposed magical properties. In the absence of a precise historical context, these last interpretations, have been favoured.

> The diminutive size and the miniature inscription of the stamps together with their smooth, fine-grained, distinctively-coloured stones generally chosen for their manufacture made them eye-catching, tactile, and eminently portable objects. But their dyes must have made them much more than attractive trinkets. In use as markers for healing medicaments, the complicated and abbreviated Latin jargon would probably have impressed those who sought cures of healers. Indeed, it is not improbable that the stamps were regarded rather as a professional attribute, the healer's badge of office, perhaps, irrespective of whether or not his level of literacy matched that implied by the stamp. However, once taken out of their medical context, in time or place, and set in the hands of those who were illiterate or were not conversant with the codified Latin texts, they may well have come to be regarded with more than awe: they may have been imbued with mysterious powers ... It is distinctly possible, therefore, that some were re-used as talismans, charms and amulets, no less precious in antiquity for their metamorphosis, but potentially misleading today in terms of their lost patterns.[9]

Not much progress, indeed, from the idea of a 'cunning medieval leech' proposed in the first report in the *Archaeological Journal*. But while one century and a half ago interpretations like this could be justified on the very little evidence and understanding of the Roman material in Ireland, they appear now totally inconsistent with our knowledge of a progressive, and by the fourth century, massive Romanisation of the country. This is not an alien intrusion but simply a rare object. In the specific case it cannot be said that the object is of uncertain attribution (it is a distinctive Roman object) nor can it be said that it is unprovenanced (it has been found together with human bones, though unfortunately dispersed when the excavation took place). Why propose that it changed its original, well-known, destination only because it does not fit the traditional picture of an untouched Ireland?

The only legitimate question then is whether the oculist stamp was used by an itinerant doctor or by a military one. The hypothesis of itinerant doctors using oculist stamps makes a lot of sense. Instead of carrying with them fragile and bulky containers for the more than 30 remedies mentioned in the existing oculist stamps, the eye doctors would incorporate these remedies in portable tablets prior to starting their usual circuits and use them in a diluted form according to need. This hypothesis is supported by the discovery of such stamps in places evenly spread throughout Britain. Furthermore, they come with virtually no exception, from sites located on the main Roman road network. If the Tipperary oculist stamp belongs to an itinerant doctor, one comes to the surprising conclusion that Ireland was part of that network and that organised medical activities were carried out there, which in all probability originated in Britain. Quite a daring conclusion, and perhaps we do not need to go so far. The alternative hypothesis of a military eye doctor seems, in fact, more plausible and better reflects the uniqueness of the find.

We know that soldiers in the Roman army suffered eye diseases. They must have had their own eye doctors, and oculist stamps have been found at fortresses and forts both on the continent and in Britain. Of the 30 British findings, however, only three came from military sites, three were discovered at villa sites, a further three at rural sites, and the rest are from towns.[10]

This is enough, it is argued, to support the use of oculist stamps both by itinerant civilian and by military doctors but not enough to suggest an exclusive or priority use of such stamps by military doctors alone.

Numbers are numbers, but it must be said that the idea of towns, where civil activities were carried out, as being totally distinct from fortresses which were centres for military activities, is far from clear cut. Military and civil affairs were, in fact, often run in British Roman towns, which always retained a distinct military character. Most towns had originated from Roman military camps and, by the end of the second century, many British towns had their own defences, a situation without parallel elsewhere in the empire. Local militia bands, and perhaps, towards the end of the empire, mercenary troops guaranteed their defence, but the overall responsibility for such defence remained, almost to the end, with the Roman army.

This intermingling of civil and military, and often religious, activities in towns where oculist stamps were found is confirmed by continental examples, the most excellent of all being the French Mandeure, the archaeological cradle of oculists' stamps. Here in 1606, the first of such objects was brought to light, the first of a long series of nine, making Mandeure the third town in the Roman world with regard to the number of this type of find. Although Madeure originated as a sanctuary and developed as a thermal town, this development was largely favoured by its strategic military position at the watershed of the Rhône and Rhine. Hence a high military presence and frequentation was probable, both for defensive and for religious purposes, since the sanctuary is likely to have been dedicated to the god of war, Mars.[11] A similar situation may have occurred in most of the British towns where oculist stamps were found, reinforced by the fact that a military presence, in some of them, was important. By contrast in London, the only real civilian metropolis in Roman Britain, only one oculist stamp has been found despite the size of the city.

If the hypothesis of military doctors is the first choice, but not the exclusive one, for users of oculist's stamps in Britain and the empire, it seems to provide the only reasonable explanation in the case of the Tipperary oculist stamp. We do not have here, as in Britain, other findings in urban conglomerations, nor have we, urban conglomerations at all. The origin of the stamp can only be military and, as such, greatly contributes to the emerging picture of a Roman invasion of Ireland.

A LONG WAY TO TIPPERARY

The natural landing sites of any journey moving from Britain across the

Irish Sea towards the south of Ireland are in the Cork and Waterford areas. In the ninth and twelfth centuries these were to be the entry points respectively for the Viking and Norman invasions in the region and were most likely the entry points of the Roman expedition that ended in County Tipperary. The estuaries of the Rivers Lee and Suir offer excellent harbours and easy access to the hinterland. Which one was chosen by the Roman invading force? Which route did they follow to reach County Tipperary? How much time did it take to complete their voyage?

Sixty miles away from the coast, the Rock of Cashel would be reached in a four-day march following, in all probability, the same route as the present N24 road from Waterford to Limerick or the road N20 from Cork to Limerick, with an eastern detour at Mallow along roads N73 and N8. In the fourth century AD these roads were not, of course, there but the passage along the River Suir west of Waterford, and that along the valleys between the mountains north of Cork, gave the easiest access to the Tipperary area.

If they moved along the Suir, the Roman troops may have made a first stop somewhere in the Carrick-on-Suir area where County Waterford ends, to enter County Tipperary the following day. Another day's march would have been necessary to reach the present Clonmel, a stronghold ever since and, interesting in the context of our story, the place where Bane, a sergeant of the local police, lived, who found the oculist stamp at Golden in 1842. Remember, Golden is also on the Suir. The most likely stop for the invading troops would have been at Cahir. The small island in the middle of the River Suir at Cahir was certainly a strategic point since ancient times, and the *Book of Lecan* tells us of the destruction of a fort here as early as the third century.

No Roman finds have yet been discovered along this ideal route from Waterford to Cashel to support this hypothesis, but the picture changes completely if at the junction of the Rivers Barrow and Suir in Waterford estuary, we follow the first, rather than the second river, proceed further north into County Kilkenny and reach the small town of Stoneyford on the River Nore. It changes completely here because, at the end of this alternative route, the remains of a Roman classical burial were found in 1852.

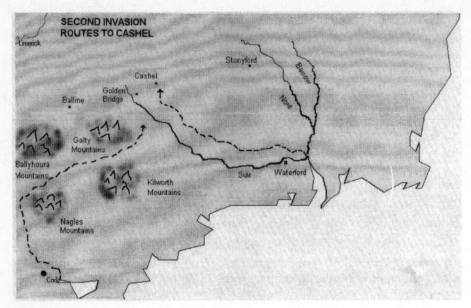

Map 6.

A scrapbook by the antiquarian Edward Clibborn, now in the Royal Irish Academy, reveals that, at the moment of the find, the remains consisted of a plain, light green glass urn with human bones in it, a glass lachrymatory and a bronze circular mirror, silvered or tinned on the convex side, used as a cover to the urn. Not very far away from these three objects, three more were found: a finger ring and two toilet bronze implements. They were not treated with great love.

In 1881 the objects came into the possession of the Antiquities Division of the National Museum but, in 1902, were transferred to the Arts and Industrial Division, probably in the belief that Stoneyford could in no way be a Roman burial site and that all six objects were 'intruders' to be preserved only as examples of Roman glass production. In 1914, the urn was smashed to pieces when the case containing it fell over and the neck of the lachrymatory was perhaps also broken and lost on that occasion. The objects were abandoned in this state for decades until, very recently, Bourke, a freelance archaeologist, started inquiring about them. The urn was at last 'happily rediscovered' and reconstructed eventually to join the other finds at the Antiquities Division of the Museum.[12] This treatment was in harsh contrast with the likely importance of such finds.

> Those who carried out the interment were obviously familiar with the process of first- or second-century Roman burial ritual. This and the possibility that it was a female [the grave goods suggest that this may have been the burial of a woman], along with the presence of a delicate and fragile glass urn, suggest that we have here evidence of a Roman presence more permanent than would be explained merely by occasional trading contacts. In this light, the location of Stoneyford may be particularly significant, as Richard Warner suggested, for it lies not far from a crossing of the River Nore and within easy reach of Waterford harbour. The possibility that a Roman trading station existed somewhere in the area merits consideration.[13]

If a Roman trading station was present in the region already two centuries before our history, the possibility of a second invasion moving from Waterford along the River Suir appears quite solid. Even more solid, perhaps, is the alternative that the invasion started with a landing in the Cork area.

In terms of native production the south of Ireland had been for centuries an archaeological desert, a desert progressively filled with material of Roman origin. While Roman finds of the first and second centuries AD primarily concentrated in the Dublin and in the north-eastern areas, the south-eastern region becomes prominent, particularly in the Cork area, in the fourth and fifth centuries. The Cork Public Museum exhibits a Roman *fibula* of the first century AD and a small bronze brooch of a Roman fourth-century AD type. But many Roman coins have also been found scattered all around the Cork area and in the forts of Garranes and Garryduff, near Cork, an amazing selection of Roman pottery and Roman-inspired objects have also been discovered.

Unlike the first invasion, however, finds have not only a coastal connotation. They are found, as the examples of Golden, Balline and Stoneyford clearly show, well inside the country, hinting at a different type of Roman intrusion. Instead of an occasional expedition in a still

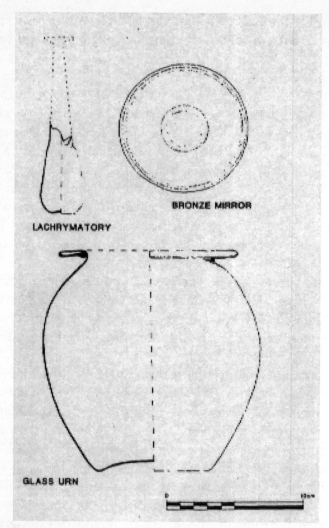

Figure 12. Finds from a first-century Roman burial in Ireland (Stoneyford).

largely unknown country limiting itself to little more than the landing sites, the finds seem to indicate familiarity with the country and the capacity of moving quickly into a relatively known hinterland. Centuries of contacts and trade were making a second invasion a much easier one logistically but also a completely different one in many respects since the interplay between Ireland and the Roman empire had greatly developed and changed in the meantime.

ACROSS THE IRISH SEA

On the other side of the Irish Sea, in Wales, Romans were reinforcing their defences against an escalation of Irish raids. Late fortifications at the fleet-base of Holyhead in the fourth century are evidence of this strategic change. Also in the fourth century Romans reoccupied Carmarthen and built a new fort at Cardiff. Two Roman signal stations at Martinhoe and Old Burrow on the south side of the Bristol Channel confirm the key defensive role of this area. Times were tough indeed for the Romans.

Troubles had started to become serious at the death of Constantine in AD 337. Under his rule there had been no real dangers for the empire, but the situation changed quickly with his successors, starting with Constans who in AD 343, for unknown reasons but certainly not for pleasure, had to rush to Britain in deep winter. As a consequence of his visit, an initial plan for a re-fortification of cities in Britain was perhaps started. It seems that the emperor also managed to gain a commitment from the most bellicose tribes in Scotland and Ireland to abstain from future raids.

The agreement lasted for a while, but in AD 360 the Scots and Picts broke their promise, and started looting various regions of Britain. Julian, Caesar for Gaul and Britain, sent his commander-in-chief, Lupicinus, to put down the insurrection. The decade that followed was characterised by repeated attacks until, in AD 367, something happened that dramatically changed the traditional scene. Tribes which had for centuries fought each other, thus allowing the Romans to apply the rule *divide et impera,* conspired together in what Ammianus Marcellinus calls the *barbarica conspiratio* and attacked the empire. It was a disaster. Hordes of Picts from Scotland, Scots from Ireland, Attacotti also from Ireland or from the Western Isles, went on a rampage. Fullofaudes, the commander of the Roman army in Britain, was killed, and it took years for the newly-appointed commander, Teodosius, to re-establish order and consolidate his defences.

Another victim of the conspiracy was Nectaridus, chief of the maritime region and in charge of the Saxon shore forts and, most probably, of the forts on the west coast, including the one in Cardiff.

Nectaridus' authority in 367 may well have included both sides of the Channel and its scope been large enough to require an officer of the rank of a *comes*, as understood in Valentinian's day. The command may still have been an 'ad hoc' one. It is possible, in fact, that Nectaridus had been appointed to lead a task force specifically to clear out pirates, either by Valentinian or even by Julian at some time after the hasty recall of Lupicinus in the winter of 360-61, perhaps in response to the raids recorded for 364.[14]

The fact that Nectaridus was not apparently replaced confirms that his appointment was of a particular nature, meeting a special threat such as the Irish raids on the western coast of Britain. If this was the case and he attacked Ireland in a retaliatory expedition landing in the Cork or Waterford areas, the most likely departure site would have been in South Wales around the Bridgewater Bay and the mouth of the Severn.

For centuries the legionary fortress of *Isca,* Caerleon, on the navigable estuary of the Usk had dominated the scene here. However, by the second half of the fourth century, the time of our story, the legion had probably left, though Roman troops were still occupying the site. But, not far away, in Cardiff, a new fortress was being built at this very time. A perfect square of almost 200 by 200 metres, armed externally with semi-octagonal projecting bastions, the Cardiff fortress was the Roman response to the increasing dangers in this area from overseas. Its remnants are still there, swollen by a late nineteenth-century horror, the reconstruction known as Cardiff Castle. It took two to make this pastiche, the third marquess of Bute and his architect, 'highly talented dreamers who sought to recreate their visions of the Middle Ages in their own lifetimes'.[15] Its only advantage now is that we can have a visual idea of the strength of this Roman fortress, the most probable base for an expedition to Ireland under Nectaridus' command.

The troops led by Nectaridus would be quite different from those who accompanied Agricola in the first expedition. Their backbone would

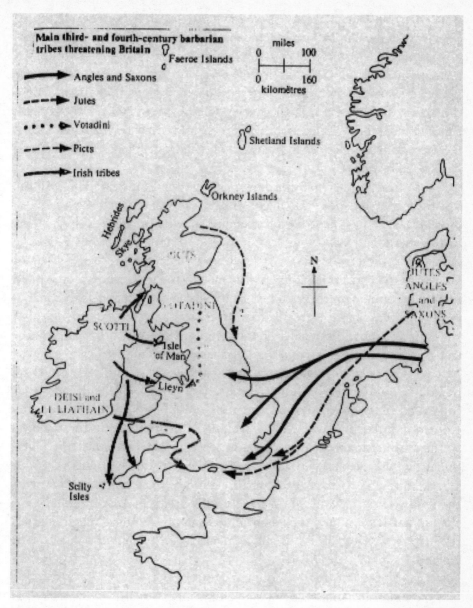

Map 7. Main third- and fourth-century barbarian tribes threatening Britain.

still consist of Roman citizens (Roman citizenship had been granted to all *cives* within the empire since Caracalla times) but barbarian units would now form the greater part of the expedition army. These would almost certainly include Germans (Nectaridus was himself a German) who were excellent warriors with no strong national sentiment that could pose a threat to the empire, together with troops of Irish origin. As with Agricola, members of defeated Irish tribes and dispossessed kings would most probably play a role in the invasion. This time their role could have been a major one.

The attack of this invasion force, highly mobile and familiar with the territory to be invaded, was likely to be a swift and conclusive one. The area of Cashel must have been reached in a few days, the local Irish chiefs dispossessed and new *foederati* leaders put into power instead. The Roman invading troops must have withdrawn soon after, in any case not later than the end of the military season. But the Irish who accompanied them were to remain there and to establish a new Romano-Irish connection. This was in turn greatly reinforced by the fact that the defeated tribes had to move elsewhere, possibly those parts of Wales facing southeast Ireland, joining previous Irish settlements established there. It was perhaps the only time in history when the Irish Sea fully deserved its name being inhabited on both sides by Irish people. In the decades that followed, it became a natural area of cross-fertilisation between the Roman and the Irish world. This included Christianity and the building of the Irish national identity. Some at least of the *foederati* that participated in the second invasion were likely to be Christians, since Christianity was by then the official religion of the empire, and many of the Irish settlers in Wales must have been Christians. Not by chance are the pre-Patrician saints, such as Brid of Kildare, Ciarán of Saigir, Déclan of Ardmore, Aibe of Emly, all associated with southern districts of Ireland.

> The Irish sea was the centre of one cultural area, 'The Irish Sea Province', as it has been called, in which relationships between eastern Ireland and western Britain were often closer than between east and west Ireland.[16]

Was all this the exclusive consequence of Nectaridus' expedition? Could the history of Ireland be re-written on the basis of one single military episode? And, most importantly, what are the arguments in favour of our story as opposed to the official one?

AN ALTERNATIVE HISTORY

The 'official' story is that a Munster tribe, the Desii, moved to Wales at some point during the first centuries of the Christian area. Apart from the very existence of such a tribe, that seems confirmed by the name of the baronies of Decies in Waterford and Tipperary, the remainder are stories written during or later than the eighth century AD. It is as if we were now writing the first history of the French Revolution. Certainly there are elements of antiquity in such stories but their reliability as an historical, even if indirect, source is now totally questionable. Mythological figures, saints, kings, fantasy animals, the natural and supernatural are combined in an often fascinating but totally unsubstantiated narrative.

In our case the different versions of the story are somehow contradictory. In Cormac's *Glossary*, the Irish presence in Wales is presented as a logic of conquest: 'For when the power of the Irish over the British was great, they divided Britain among them in territories, and each knew where his allies dwelt. And there were as many Irish living in the east across the sea as there were in Ireland, and they made houses and royal fortresses there.'[17] However, another tale, significantly entitled *The expulsion of the Desii*, tells us instead of the forced migration of a dispossessed people. Dating when these events were supposed to have happened is also most confusing. The traditional view derived from lists of Irish rulers in early Irish epics, that the emigration took place in the third or fourth century, is now highly controversial. Some of the best scholars seem to agree on an initial dating at the end of the fourth century, in line with the hypothesis of a second Roman invasion to Ireland.[18]

What is certain is that Irish tribes settled in Wales at that time and began a fundamental cultural interplay with the Romans on the one hand and with Ireland on the other. The exchange was firstly a linguistic one with the Irish settlers becoming quickly bilingual as the evidence of multilingual ogham inscriptions clearly confirms. It was also a religious and material exchange that eventually moved from this unique Welsh experience into Ireland again.

> There are several features about the indigenous culture that can be seen to have resonances with that found in Early Christian Ireland. The continuance of the round house as the domestic dwelling, the use of relatively small circular or sub-rectangular enclosures which were not heavily defended, the range of agricultural and craft tools, and the lack of local ceramic production are all similar to Ireland. This is not to suggest that all these traits were copied slavishly and translated across the Irish sea. Rather, it was within this cultural environment that the Irish settled, become integrated with the local population and would have became acculturated with some at least of the Romanising traits. These traits may also have included Christianity by this time, as it certainly did in some areas of Somerset, but it is difficult to date much of the relevant material, and cist-grave cemeteries may anyway have started as a pagan burial form, as might sites that developed into church-yards.[19]

Religious material and particularly linguistic interplay can only develop and be maintained under conditions of social stability and progressive integration. The picture that emerges is one of a peaceful migration into a marginal, relatively inhabited part of the empire rather that one of war and conquest. Certainly early Irish raiders are likely to have settled in Wales well before the time of our history, but the movement of populations is another matter. It needs to be grounded in substantial reasons, such as the long history of continuous conflict among Irish tribes, and it needs a powerful shock to materialise. In our case, the shock was most likely a Roman military invasion.

According to our reconstruction a Romano-Irish army, perhaps led by Nectaridus, moved from Cardiff in the years AD 364-367, landed most probably in the Cork area and made its way through the hinterland mountains to what we now call County Tipperary and the Rock of Cashel. Archaeological evidence, the only thing available given the lack of any reliable literary source on either the Roman or the Irish side, shows an unusual concentration of Roman finds in the Cork area at that time and a limited, but significant number of finds in the Tipperary region. The Rock of Cashel takes its name from the Roman word *castrum* and has revealed in recent excavations Romano-British material. We have placenames in the region indicating the presence of a tribe, the Desii, which was most likely forced to migrate to Wales at exactly the same time. Extensive evidence in Wales confirms that this migration effectively took place and that a long period of mutual cultural exchange began, which was to influence greatly the future history of Ireland. This is our reconstruction based on the existing evidence. It may not be all the evidence we would like to have but it is the only one available at the moment. As the wise would say: better a drop of evidence than a sea of imagination.

CHAPTER 6

Traders and Geographers

ROMAN COINS IN IRELAND

Professor Michael O'Kelly was 51 years old on 21 December 1969 when he made the discovery of his life. At 9.58am of that winter solstice he observed a sunbeam passing through the stone roofbox at the passage entrance to reach across the chamber floor, the front edge of the basin stone in the end chamber. It was the final proof that what legends and traditions had been saying for centuries was true, that the neolithic tomb of Newgrange in the Boyne Valley was on a solar alignment that day of the year, that the entire monument had been built in perfect astronomical orientation, that here was the Irish response to Stonehenge. It was *the* media event within a campaign of excavations lasting fourteen years, one of the major continued efforts of Irish archaeology. It left in relative oblivion another discovery of less sensational impact but of crucial importance for the history of Ireland: an intriguing harvest of Roman coins.

Roman coins had started to appear three centuries earlier in Newgrange. The first find, a golden coin of the emperor Valentinian, was made in 1699 when the entrance of the tomb was accidentally found. Attracted by the news of the discovery the scholar Edward Lhwyd who was visiting Ireland at that time, was one of the first to access the monument and to search the area after centuries of oblivion. Another two coins were found by the antiquarian Molyneux who visited Newgrange in 1709, and three more were reported by Lord Albert Conyngham in 1842 as having been found by 'labouring men' just a few yards from the entrance. This time, five gold ornaments, with unquestionable Roman features, were also found with two bracelets, two rings and a chain, that strongly hint to much more than a casual presence. It was the beginning of a long series of Roman finds, culminating in 1967 with the discovery of the hook-end of a gold torc with an enigmatic inscription in Roman letters: SCRONS.MB, perhaps the oldest Roman inscription in Ireland.

During these three centuries the number of Roman coins found at Newgrange had grown continuously up to the current figure of 25, covering the entire period of the Roman presence in Britain, from Domitianus (AD 81-96) to Arcadius (AD 385-408). A most important collection, these coins are, however, only the tip of the iceberg. Altogether something between 2,500 and 3,000 Roman coins, including those in hoards, have been dug out of the Irish soil. An impressive number which in turn could prove to be only the tip of another iceberg, that of all the Roman coins which made their way to Ireland and were subsequently lost, transformed into other metal objects or deposited somewhere and never found again. Is there a way of guessing their total number?

For some Roman forts in Britain, Corbridge in Northumberland for instance, we know the number of years of occupation, how much each soldier was paid per year, and we have the number of coins found on the site. Now, in the case of Corbridge, the value of coin finds represents a real coin population valued at 10,000 times higher.[1]

Keeping to the example, if we consider that Corbridge was occupied for about two centuries and Roman coins in Ireland span some three centuries, we should multiply the value of the coins found there by 15,000 to establish the value of Roman coins during that period. In most cases we should stop here because the coins found are usually of little value and represent a very biased part of the coin population: 1,387 small coins in Corbridge, equivalent in value to only 26 golden coins. In the case of Ireland, however, the value of coins found is a much more balanced one, with even golden coins well represented. It is perhaps possible to go further and suggest that the coins found are somehow representative of the entire coin population and that their number multiplied by 15,000 would not only give the value but also, by some approximation, the number of the entire coin population. According to this calculation a total of 40 million Roman coins could have been entering Ireland during the period of the Roman presence in Britain. An exaggeration? Perhaps, but even with all possible caution and re-adjustments, an amazing figure and one that challenges all previous interpretations.

Among the most popular interpretations is one that, far from seeing Ireland as an area under Roman influence, looks at the island as an untouched territory and considers all finds that do not fit into this vision as spurious and alien. As far as objects are concerned this means questioning Roman features and discovering Celtic traits at all costs. In the case of coins, this questioning being impossible, the argument is that they are 'late' imports. Thus, by applying very rigorous criteria as to the context, which is often uncertain in the case of coin finds, most of them have been dismissed as original imports. This is a very drastic approach, based on the presumed 'uniqueness' of the Irish finds and on the ultimate idea of scholars, antiquarians, travellers and amateurs littering for centuries the whole of Ireland with hundreds of Roman coins, an idea that demands some verification.

Late imports of Roman coins certainly occurred in Ireland as in other parts of the empire. However, the fact that the finds are without a clear archaeological context is not simply taken as a reason for considering a coin find as a late import. It would be too simple and too easy. What is sought for, instead, is a sound criterion for distinguishing between original and late imports, usually, in the case of coins, asking whether they come from a mint not too far away or from a distant mint. To take the example of Britain, although mints as far away as those of Antioch, Alexandria and Constantinople contributed to the coinage of the country, the fact that a coin originated in a far-away mint is seen as suspicious because of the lack of an archaeological context, while if the coin was produced in home or nearby mints, such as those of London, Colchester or Trier, this is seen as a clear indication that it is not a late import.

Without an archaeological context, it is not possible to prove categorically when Roman coins arrived in an area and were lost, but in Britain it is possible to be satisfied that some Roman coins are late imports. One such case is that of the higher proportion of coins of the Roman period from eastern mints found in Glasgow, while on excavated Roman sites in Scotland the coins are, as one would expect, overwhelmingly from the western mints, particularly Trier. While some people have in the past tried to see some contemporary significance to the abnormal Glasgow representation, it is now recognised that this distribution has more to do with souvenirs brought back by travellers and soldiers than to the activities of the Romans in Scotland. The very low proportions of eastern coins on excavated sites must provide the likely 'normal' level of the representation of such coins in Scotland.[2]

In the case of Ireland, not only were the vast majority of coin finds in circulation in Britain but most of them originated in perfectly acceptable mints according to the above criterion. Going back to the case of Newgrange, the coins of which have been studied in depth, all the golden coins, except one, are from the Trier mint, while other mints represented are all western ones: London, Rome, Amiens, Cologne and Milan. This evidence is consistent with a context of original imports from Britain and other nearby parts of the empire. But why and who introduced these coins into Ireland?

Soldiers and merchants, it has been suggested, used them for a variety of purposes. Most of the coins belong to hoards: the Ballinrees (Coleraine) hoard with its 1,506 *siliquae,* the Feigh Mountain hoard composed of at least 500 coins, the Flower Hill hoard comprising 300 coins, to cite only the major ones. But hoards as such are just accumulations of coins, and the reasons for such accumulations can be numerous. As we have seen, hoards could be gathered as the result of looting, as a reserve of valuables, for melting purposes by foundrymen, by merchants burying them at strategic locations along their itinerary, or constituting ransom money to stop raiders' incursions, or as payment for military services. The traditional image of a hoard as a heap of coins without context gives way progressively to the understanding that hoards, and those that consisted of Roman coins, were fulfilling a series of functions in the social context of Ireland.

Roman coins were probably also used for other purposes. Some were most likely votive offerings, particularly in sacred centres, as the examples of Newgrange and Tara seem to suggest.

Although there was no money-using economy in Ireland at that period, Roman coins did find their way to Ireland, just as they did to other areas bordering the empire. There is a considerable record of Roman coins found in Ireland either in the form of hoards or as more isolated finds, the result of casual loss. Neither of these categories provides a satisfactory explanation for the present finds [those of Newgrange]. While the two asses of Domitian on their own might be explicable as casual losses, the very quantity of coins, let alone the high value of a good many, rules out loss as an adequate explanation. It is equally clear from the wide date range and the scattered find-spots that a hoard is not in question ... The theory that Roman coins at least were deposited as offerings appear and, indeed, may well turn out to be a far-fetched one, but to date it is the only one which at all fits the facts.[3]

Further functions must have included burial practices, as the seven skeletons and their coins buried along the Bray shore indicate. Another 150 coins, scattered all around Ireland, call for even wider and more diversified functions. Some of these functions clearly coincide with those of a normal currency.

A symbolic function, first of all, is typical of several native currencies and also of modern coins and notes, which often reflects the power of the issuing authority and, therefore, the status of the owner of the currency itself. Not many Irish, perhaps, would have known the name of the ruling emperor portrayed on Roman coins, though some, such as merchants and soldiers who served in the Roman army, certainly did. Even this memory would have been lost in a few generations while Roman coins continued to be on the Irish scene for centuries. But people would still recognise in these coins, even if in an indirect and vague way, the power and symbols of Rome. Something like the thaler with the portrait of Maria Thérèse of Austria which continued to be coined with the date 1780 for exclusive use in the vast regions of north-eastern Africa until the Second World War.

Populations in these regions would load these coins with symbolic significance and would refuse to use new currency which had been introduced in the meantime. The same would be true, with all due distinction, for the owner of a gold or silver Roman coin in Ireland, and we can well imagine the impact of the portraits of Roman emperors represented on such coins, and of figures from the classical world on their reverse, on the Irish imagination. It is likely that a number of elements of Irish myths and legends as well as of Irish symbolism in art originated here.

Ornamental functions are also often associated with currency. Among the natives in Oceania shell-currency and shell-ornament were so closely linked that it is difficult to say which came first. The use of coins as an ornament has been a tradition for centuries in the vast region from the Balkans to India and is now widespread in the entire Western world. This must have been the case in Ireland too, as the two Roman gold coins from Newgrange which were transformed into pendants clearly show. But in Ireland the association went even further. Roman coins are often found mixed with other ornaments, and it is generally assumed that a great part of Roman coins which reached the country were melted and converted into such ornaments. The gold and silver of some of the masterpieces of Irish metalwork most probably originated from such coins.

Finally, Roman coins were considered for their intrinsic value. Unlike in other places in the empire, where finds of Roman coins are typically pieces of little value, in Ireland coins of precious metal represent a very substantial part of such finds. It is likely that, as for other currencies, they were used in trade or commerce, though they had probably to be assayed at every exchange. Other pieces of precious metal, such as the silver ingots of Balline, are also likely to have had monetary functions, as seen in the previous chapter, and seem to confirm a panorama where Roman coins and ingots, and precious metal objects derived from them, were the centre of an intriguing interplay among symbolic, personal and economic elements very similar to that which normally characterises currencies.

We are far away from the idea of looting, isolated late imports and casual loss, even if Roman coins were never used in Ireland as a general medium of exchange in the same way as a normal modern currency would be.

What appears increasingly evident is that the role of Roman coins in Ireland was much more important than has been for long believed. In the monetary vacuum in which Ireland found itself from its pre-history well into its history, these coins were for centuries the only thing that most resembled and, to a large extent, fulfilled the functions of a real currency. It took a long time for the first Irish coins to be minted. When it happened, in AD 994, under the ruling of the Norse king of Dublin, Sitric Silkbeard, the coins were copied from the Crux type of Aethelred II, then in production in England. This was in turn influenced by Roman prototypes; thus the profile effigy on the obverse of the Irish coins bears clear elements of its derivation from Roman coins of the fourth century. As the Irish coinage becomes rapidly illiterate, these Roman elements somehow gain in significance to remain as a kind of popular leitmotif throughout the Irish Middle Ages and continue to inspire artists and story tellers.

TRADING BEYOND THE LIMITS OF THE EMPIRE

However important, coins were only a part of the scene in an empire that extended its trade as far as Arabia, Persia and India. Romans were left astonished by the Indian embassies who reached the capital of the empire during the kingdoms of Eliogabalus (AD 218-222), Julianus (AD 331-336) and Justinanus (AD 527-565), and Roman coins are still kept in the museums of Calcutta and Chennai where nobody would dream of considering them occasional losses. An incredible array and variety of products were imported. All kinds of spices, drugs and cosmetic products; hides, wool, linen, cotton and silk; purple-dyed clothes and ivory; slaves and eunuchs; amber and incense; exotic and wild beasts for the arenas. The significance of these goods vis-à-vis more traditional precious metals was also changing. When in AD 408 Alaric, king of the Goths, besieged Rome he demanded a ransom that included not only gold and silver but, for the first time, 3,000 scarlet dyed hides, 4,000 silk tunics and 3,000 pounds of pepper.

Ireland had its part in this trade. Roman merchants must have known its shores well since the classical age of Ptolemy, a Greek cartographer

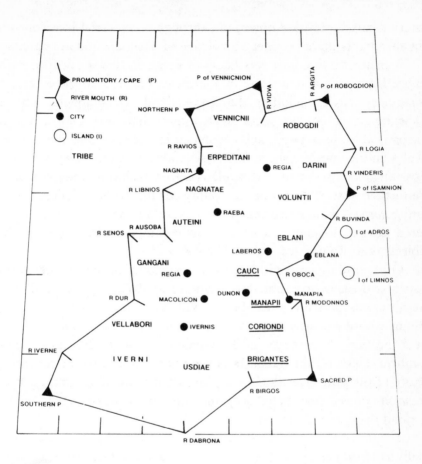

Map 8. Ptolemy map of Ireland.

based in Alexandria, who was able in the second century AD to produce a most famous 'map' of Ireland, more precisely the latitude, longitude and names of 60 features, including fifteen mouths of rivers, five promontories, eleven towns and nine islands. An astonishing achievement, the best geographical account for centuries to come since, apart from a few sketches on the back of the *Book of Kells*, it was only in the thirteenth century that better cartographic representations appeared. Even before Ptolemy, Tacitus, referring to Ireland, had written: 'The

121

interior parts are little known, but through commercial intercourse and the merchants there is better knowledge of harbours and approaches.'

A major trading post was likely to be on the coast north of Dublin, in the Damastown area. Here in a strategic position, at the centre of an imaginary circle including Lambay Island, Drumanagh, Tara and Newgrange, a copper ingot was found that was almost certainly exchanged for local goods and originated from the mining areas of North Wales on the opposite shore, where several similar examples were found. Possibly also associated with trade is a Roman bronze ladle found a little further west, in Bohermeen, County Meath. Ladles, skillets, strainers and *paterae* (a kind of saucepan) of Roman origin or derivation are scattered around Ireland as part of a wide-ranging selection of everyday objects with Roman features or inspiration.

Other trading posts most probably developed around Stoneyford and Cork, two easily accessible areas with clear Roman presence. But their number was possibly much bigger and their spread much wider than thought until recently, as a small but significant find recently discovered at a location as far away as Ballyshannon, County Donegal, seems to confirm. Here, on the outskirts of the town, about 200 metres from the shore of the Erne river estuary, a grave-digger found, in 1995, a Roman *denarius* buried one metre deep in a cluster of mussel shells on rising ground overlooking the sea.[4]

The *denarius* find revived the memories of another find fished out of Ballyshannon Bay one century ago, a sword hilt of Gaulish or British origin.[5] It also revived the memory of a passage in the *Annals of the Four Masters,* recording that in ancient times there was a Roman settlement, Eastran, at the mouth of the river Eske, just a few kilometres north of Ballyshannon. The *Annals,* a seventeenth-century compilation based on old legends, are not the most reliable reference for historical events, but the *Guide to Geography* of Ptolemy is. Although sometimes incomplete and even misleading for faraway countries, the information he provides is quite accurate for Mediterranean and European countries. His map of the world, based on the immense documentation of the library of Alexandria and even more on firsthand reports from the shipmasters berthed in that metropolis, was to be the most authoritative geographical source for almost a millennium. If one looks, in particular, at Ptolemy's map of Ireland, a position is indicated for the mouth of a river, referred to as the Ravius river, which surprisingly coincides with that of the estuary of the river Erne. The name of the river is not the same, most of Ptolemy names are different from modern ones, and the latitude and longitude do not exactly match, but Ptolemy's first meridian was in the Canaries rather than at Greenwich, and the position of his parallels reflected that of an earth's circumference supposed to be about a third shorter than it is in reality. The coincidence confirms that this was a known and frequented landing area giving easy access to the entire hinterland of northern Ireland. Here, according to legend, Partholan had landed from Scythia in about 1,500BC to begin the first colonisation of Ireland and here merchants from the Roman world are likely to have landed before Ptolemy's time and possibly to have established a trading post. Based on the Ballyshannon example, we can perhaps venture to say that others of the geographical features in Ptolemy's map could in fact indicate or be somehow related to Roman commercial settlements along the coasts of Ireland, even in locations very distant from those that have been usually considered suitable for Roman landings. But what objects and goods were traded there? And by what means of transport?

EXCHANGING DOGS FOR WINE

Wine, olive oil, amphorae, tableware, dogs, brooches, grain, copper, tin, gold, cattle and slaves, were most probably the main goods traded between Rome and Ireland. On the Irish side, wine was certainly among the favourites on the list. Although Ireland has been designated as a wine producer by the European Commission only since 1999, in the sense that the content of its little more than 5,000 bottles can now be officially called wine, local production must always have been in existence, if the great English historian Bede (AD 672-735) is to be believed that 'it does not lack vineyards'. Importation, however, has always been the primary source since very ancient times. We have seen that among the earliest Latin loan words is *fin-vinum* (wine) and also *esarn-exhibernum,* year-old wine, and the words *Bordgal, Burdigala,* Bordeaux are recurrent place names, particularly in the Westmeath area. At the Hill of Tara a goblet and sherd from several flagons of the first-second centuries AD have been found. Not far away, at Lagore crannóg, the staves of a barrel have been discovered which could have been inspired by Roman models.

The advent of Christianity certainly did not stop this trade. Wine was necessary for liturgical purposes and wine merchants must have been following missionaries into the new countries to be evangelised. The quantity of wine involved in this appears, however, sometimes rather in excess of what was strictly needed for religious purposes. In the sixth century, St Ciarán was visited in his celebrated abbey of Clonmacnoise on the river Shannon by Gaulish traders who presented him with a great quantity, *ingentem vas,* of their wine to be eventually distributed among his monks.[6] Half a century later, when St Colomba left Nantes for Ireland, he was given a gift of 200 hogshead of wheat, 100 hogshead of beer and 100 hogshead of wine, a quantity sufficient to guarantee mass celebrations for many years to come.

The importance, antiquity and continuity of wine trade between the Roman world and Ireland was highlighted in a series of lectures given by H. von Zimmer to the Prussian Royal Academy of Sciences in 1909 and 1910, where he concluded that:

Leaving for the moment aside the supposition that since older times, before west-Gaul had the capacity of exporting its own wine, traded wines reached Ireland by a transit traffic originating from Marseilles via west Gaul ports like Corbilo – it is possible that since the fourth century BC Marseilles actively traded with south-west Britain and Ireland via west-Gaul ports ... nothing can be sensibly argued against the supposition that the sixth to twelfth century, well documented, direct wine trade from west-Gaul ports to all parts of Ireland that were reachable from the coast, goes back into the first century AD at a time when west Gaul had its own wine production for export. It is evident that the export of west Gaul wines towards Ireland was more important in the twelfth century than in the sixth century and that in turn this last one was more important than the one of the first century.[7]

On the Roman side, Irish dogs were highly sought after. These were not pet dogs nor herd dogs but the most terrible slaughter dogs, *archu,* of Irish sagas and tales. They were used in battle and capable of resisting the combined attack of two warriors. Their life was valued exactly the same as a man's, as the story of the hero *Cú Chulainn,* the Hound of Culann, clearly indicates. *Cú Chulainn* had an adventurous encounter with one of these dogs when he was a young man. The dog belonged to the smith Culann and had to be kept on a chain by three men. A threat for everyone, but not our hero who made 'minced meat' of the dog! Incidentally, the Irish used to eat dogs and even engaged in chewing their meat in foretelling rituals, if we are to believe the ninth-century commentator Cormac. Chulann, however, was not very happy with the outcome of this epic gesture so the young hero had to accept to serve him as a guard-dog, hence the origin of his name, until a new pup had grown up who could in turn take his place. The celebration of *archu* which has survived through the ages, is still alive in Irish poetry.

HOUND OF THE HEROES

Huge hound
Great hound
Grey Hound and gaunt
Royally imperial
You tower above taunt.

Comrade of chieftain
Grim dog of war
Your fame has been heralded
And hailed from afar.

From Rome of the Caesars
From Spain's classic bard
You've won kingly praises
And knightly award.

The elk of old Erin
You brought to his knees
At the roar of your challenge
The timber wolf flees.

Yet noble descendant
Of fierce fighting sire
You are playing tonight
With my child by the fire.

William Dammarell[8]

Romans were very keen on exotic animals which were imported from all over the world. The import of Irish dogs was part of this trade and was already flourishing at the time of Strabo *(c.* 60 BC- *c.* AD 20). In the fourth century AD Quintus Aurelius Symmachus wrote to his brother Flavianus, thanking him for the present of seven Irish hounds. One century later St Patrick escaped from slavery in Ireland in a ship apparently loaded with these dogs.

Slaves were an important commodity in the Roman empire, but providing them was not an easy matter after the establishment of *pax Romana* throughout the entire empire. Occasionally the repression of rebellions and local wars could provide a great number of slaves but not enough to satisfy the long-term maintenance of a slave population that in Rome alone, at the time of Augustus, amounted to more than a quarter of the total population. Self-propagation, by slaves giving birth to new slaves, was the normal way, though apparently an insufficient one. The rest had to be found elsewhere in those areas at the borders of the empire where law and order were difficult to enforce. Beyond those borders, as in the case of Ireland, the slave trade must have been even more active and have played a major role in the total trade exchange.

At Lagore an intriguing selection of chains and collars has been discovered, similar to Roman specimens of the same type, which have been interpreted as slave chains or chains for hound dogs. The alternative sounds at least puzzling nowadays but, as we have seen, the value of one of the best exemplars of such dogs equalled that of a human being.

AMPHORAE AND TABLEWARE

Despite sparse indications, the real significance of trade between the empire and Ireland had remained largely a matter of speculation until, on 9 June 1942, Sean P. Ó Ríordáin presented to the Royal Irish Academy the results of his excavation of the ring fort of Garranes in Cork, a magic area for the quality and quantity of its finds and the understanding of the Romano-Hibernian interactions.

In the fort he found the most spectacular collection of Roman or sub-Roman pottery ever discovered in Ireland. It includes 40 fragments of red tableware, seven cream to grey sherds of what he referred to as 'cooking pots' and about 200 fragments of small amphorae, *lagenae*. At that time very little was known about the origin, nature and whereabouts of such pottery, but Ó Ríordáin knew of similar finds having been dug out of a number of trial holes at the nearby ring forts of Garryduff and at the important excavations at Tintagel in Cornwall in the 1930s. C.A. Raleigh Radford, who had unearthed thousands of sherds there, fully confirmed Ó Ríordáin's emerging idea that this was material directly imported from Gaul as part of a direct trade exchange between the continent and Ireland in the sixth century AD.

> It appears likely that both the Garranes and Tintagel sites owe these wares to intercourse with the Continent and, because of the absence of the closely similar wares from the Roman sites in Britain in general, it would appear that intercourse with the Continent was direct from Southern Ireland and Cornwall. We are, therefore, inclined to see in this pottery evidence for trade connections between the Cork coast and the Continent in Roman and sub-Roman times. It seems probable that these connections were directed to the coast of Gaul from whence possibly oil or wine may have imported in the lagenae represented among the Garranes pottery.[9]

Sixty years and various classifications later, we know much more about this material but opinions are still divergent and sometimes controversial.

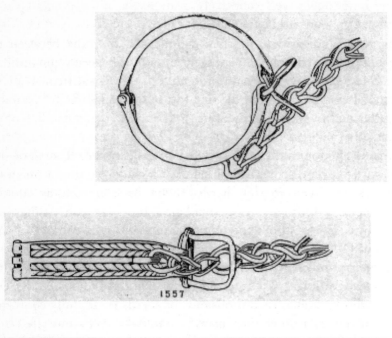

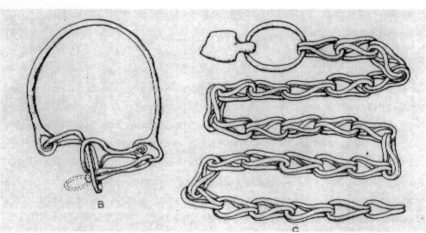

Figure 13. Slave chains and collars from Lagore.

Within this ongoing debate a new picture emerges where Roman pottery in Ireland is no longer seen exclusively as an insular affair but as a reflection of the often underestimated size of trade within and beyond the limits of the Roman empire.

Finds similar to those of the Garranes pottery have multiplied both in Britain and Ireland. Archaeologists have been able to trace nearly 400 vessels (not sherds!), 85 of which came from Ireland. We also know that these vessels came in from further away than originally believed. The red tableware (now classified as A ware) has either an African origin, probably from the Carthage region in Tunisia, or a Turkish one, from Phocis, halfway between Smyrna and Pergamon. The kitchenware (now classified as E ware) has a Gaulish origin, probably from northern or western France. The amphorae (now classified as B ware) have either an Aegean (Bi type) or a Cyprian, perhaps Egyptian (Type Bii) or a Tunisian origin (Bv type). In other words, this pottery originated in the four corners of the empire. It has even been suggested that ships carrying amphorae could have originated in Constantinople itself.[10]

Bi amphorae have also been found in Cyrenaica, Romania, Athens and Istanbul; Bii amphorae in Cyrenaica, Palestine, Tunisia, Italy, Spain, Istanbul and the Black Sea region; Bv amphorae were spread around practically the entire Mediterranean region, particularly in Rome and Ostia.[11] When these amphorae reached Ireland, and reached it in so many places as to make it impossible to subscribe the minimalist view of sporadic shipments, it meant that it had become an integral part of the immense trade network of the empire. But when had this trade started? The traditional view that Gaulish ware was imported between AD 400 and 700 and that North African and eastern Mediterranean imports took primarily place in the late fifth and sixth centuries, is now challenged.

Not the least interesting facet of recent pottery studies has been the suggestion that some of these 'post-Roman' imports may have been foreshadowed, or may have had relevant predecessors, before circa 450 – even before circa 400, and thus belong to that uncertain phase which involves the later third, fourth and earlier fifth centuries AD.[12]

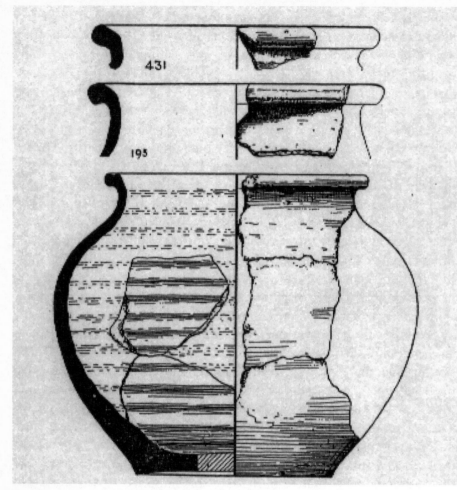

Figure 14. Roman kitchenware found in Ireland.

Pre-dating 'post-Roman' pottery not only implies making it 'Roman' but also questioning the very foundation of established assumptions concerning the dating of ring forts and *crannógs* which for long have been considered exclusively early Christian in character. This has met strong opposition, but growing questioning is based on the increasing awareness of the limits of written sources and of the reliability of the stylistic analy-

sis of metalwork as primary sources for accurate dating. Moving traditional dating backwards would also re-balance what increasingly appears
as an unnatural disproportion between the practical inexistence of Iron
Age sites as against the overabundance of early Christian sites. As already
seen it has been authoritatively suggested that a number of Irish sites,
usually dated to the second half of the first millennium AD may well have
to be back-dated into the first half of the millennium.

Looking further back is not only possible but necessary. Other types
of pottery, which are without doubt Roman and of the first and second
centuries AD, are present in Ireland. Sherds of Samian ware, a fine bright
red pottery originating in Gaul (a more refined version of the tableware
found at Garranes), have been found in several places, from Lagore, Tara
and Knowth, County Meath to Dalkey, County Dublin, from Dundrum
and Lough Faughan, County Down to Island Machugh and Clogher,
County Tyrone, including, of course, the Drumanagh site. In a few other
places, like the Ballinderry crannóg, County Offaly, sherds of Arretine
ware have been found. Originating from Arezzo, hence its name, this type
of ware dates further back to the period between 30 BC and AD 20 – a
disturbing presence which is difficult to accept.

> Considerable debate has been generated by these Roman sherds, their func-
> tions being claimed as decorative inlays, as relics or souvenirs of Rome. The
> rarity of Roman material in Ireland suggests that such finds in Early
> Christian contexts are late imports and may have a symbolic significance;
> Liversage considered that they were charms.[13]

We have already dealt with the argument of late imports or alien
entries. Unless this flow of Roman ware during various centuries is arti-
ficially split into parts and each part considered in isolation, there is no
way of contradicting the evidence that it reached Ireland as part of an
expanding interchange with the Roman world. Again, as for many other
aspects, it was a natural osmotic process rather than the sudden awakening of trade at the dawn of the Christian era.

BOATS AND ROADS

The process must have progressively influenced the inner parts of Ireland with merchants introducing not only Roman goods but also Roman techniques and, ultimately, aspects of the Roman way of life into the most remote parts of the island. For inland water transport they would have used the traditional dug-out canoe. But not only those. In 1968, a boat of a different type was found in Lough Lene, County Westmeath, one of the most secluded parts of Ireland, and it appeared to be Roman.

This vessel unquestionably belongs to the Mediterranean tradition of shipbuilding. The use of mortise, tenons and pegs, as shown, has nothing to do with the Celtic way of building boats. It is the sixth example found north of the Alps, all others having been discovered in strongly Romanised contexts, and is probably second or third, but certainly not later than fourth century in date. How it reached Ireland is a mystery. Was it built there by a Roman settler or a Romanised Irish person? If this is the case (boats are not usually carried in pockets like coins and this one is too small to have crossed the open sea) the find of Lough Lene goes a long way to tell the extent of the pervading Roman influence on Irish society.

The same cannot easily be said for road transport. No Roman road has ever been found in Ireland, against about 10,000 miles in Britain, a fact that also goes far in telling us the significance and limits of the Romanisation of the island. On this evidence any connection between Roman and Irish roads had always been denied – until 1985, when the exceptional find of almost two kilometres of wooden causeway across the bog at Corlea, County Longford, showing sophisticated planning and building capacities, raised great interest in the subject and gave some ground for considering a possible Roman influence. Could Corlea be seen as an early example of indirect Romanisation? Not quite, since dates do not match. Although the first Roman consular road, the Appian way, was built in 312 BC, the construction of the Corlea causeway in 150 BC, according to dendrochronological analysis (tree-ring dating), pre-dates by two centuries the appearance of Roman roads in Britain. For an early example it is too early.

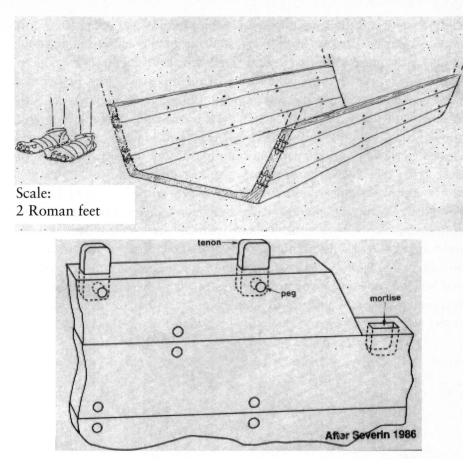

Scale:
2 Roman feet

Figure 15. A Roman boat in Ireland – a vessel known as a 'monk's boat' from Lough Lene, County Westmeath (top) and the details of mortise-tenson-joints typical of the Mediterranean tradition (bottom).

On this basis, and until a Roman road is discovered in Ireland, the argument seems closed. Not completely so, however, if we listen to a theory advanced by Kenneth Jermy, a British expert on Roman roads. For many years he has been engaged in demonstrating that *Longford* is a significant name for tracing Roman roads. In an article that appeared in the authoritative *Britannia* in 1992, Jermy showed that almost half of 52 places in England and Wales named *Longford/Langford* are within three kilometres of a Roman road, a correlation that must be better than random.[14] He also suggests that *Longford/Langford* comes from the Old English *lange* and a Celtic element *forde* which is allied to the modern Welsh *ffordd,* road, to indicate a long, straight road.[15] Now, the Corlea causeway is located in County Longford, only thirteen kilometres south of Longford town, and can certainly be described as a long, straight, ancient road – a most intriguing correlation. Did someone assimilate the Corlea causeway to a Roman road in antiquity or was the name introduced later on? The Irish county town of Longford could well be named after the now disappeared fortress *(Longphort)* of the princes of Annaly, the O'Farrels, but it could also carry in its name the memory of old, forgotten implications with the Roman world. This last may well be the right answer. As K. Jermy notes, the correlation between Roman roads and the name *Longford/Langford* becomes more important in England and Wales as one moves towards the west, the area where Celtic influence was the strongest. What is more western and Celtic than Longford town in the very heart of Ireland?

CHAPTER 7

Gods and the Other World

IN SEARCH OF RELIGIOUS SYNCRETISM

When passing the majestic columns in red-grey granite and the bronze door, modern visitors enter the Pantheon, and find themselves in an immense rotunda surrounded by alternating circular and rectangular niches, polycromous marbles and frescoed shrines. Looking above they can see the only opening of the entire building: the 'eye' dominating a cupola whose diameter of more than 43 metres is the largest in Rome, larger than the celebrated St Peter's cupola in the Vatican. A marvellous work of engineering, a masterpiece of all times, the Pantheon's dome was built by employing the most sophisticated techniques and using different materials to spread its immense weight. Visitors cannot see it, but moving towards the top the small bricks of the first part progressively give way to the use of much lighter materials such as amphorae and eventually volcanic ash. Underneath this wonder, pilgrims can nowadays visit the tomb of the painter Rafael and, surrounded by self-nominated royal guards, those of the kings of Italy.

The scene 2,000 years ago would have been quite different. Niches and shrines would be filled with the statues of a variety of gods because, as the name of the temple tells us, this was a building for the worship of all gods. Monotheism, with its intolerance and exclusion, was still to come. There was not overt conflict among the gods of the classical pantheon and the Romans favoured in general assimilation when new acquisitions were made. Visitors walking in the streets of ancient Rome in imperial times would find in the Campus of Mars the prestigious temple

135

of the Egyptian goddesses Isis and Sarapis and more than ten other temples devoted to Egyptian cults spread around the capital. So important was the temple to Isis and Serapis that the region of Rome in which it was located was named after the two goddesses instead of after the Coliseum that also stood in that area. Visitors would also find, but more hidden from public view, some 40 sanctuaries devoted to the cult of Mithras, a cult that the Christians, when in power, wiped out with ferocious determination. In the Mithras sanctuary below the S. Prisca church on the Aventine Hill, excavations revealed the presence of other gods and goddesses including Serapis,Venus and Mars as well as Hecate, Fortuna, Dionysus and Aesculapius. A similar congregation, though with different gods, would be found on the same hill in the temple of Jupiter Dolichenus, a Roman version of the Syrian god Baals. Religious tolerance, syncretism and the assimilation of new cults, particularly oriental ones, was a main feature of the Roman empire.

Gods and goddesses from all over the oriental world (Asia Minor, Egypt, Persia and Syria) were, by the first century AD, an integral part of the Roman pantheon. The Roman world originally came into contact with the eastern culture through conquest and colonisation, through oriental trade and merchants, and through eastern soldiers who made their way into their auxiliary regiments, thus being disseminated all over the empire. The oriental mystery religions had a great attraction over cults of Roman origin. Each appears to have involved a personal relationship between the individual and his god.[1]

A similar process of assimilation occurred with the gods of the Celts but in a different way. Despite the fact that close contacts between the Italic and the Celtic world pre-dated by centuries those with the oriental world, the influence of Celtic religion on Roman beliefs remained substantially a local phenomenon. This was a religion that appealed much less to Rome than oriental religions because of its uncertain connotations, and lack of iconographic representation and innovative value-messages. No temple to Celtic gods was ever erected in the capital of the empire.

Locally, however, the symbiosis was large and intense. The Celtic religion, Caesar tells us, was an all-pervasive one. Gods were many, shadowy and multi-functional. Of the 400 god names of the Romano-Celtic period, over 300 are mentioned only once.[2] Key features included the cult of sun and sky, mother and fertility goddesses, animals and animism, water-gods, war-gods, gods of the Other World, healing gods plus a strong belief in immortality together with an array of monsters, superstitions, magic and ritual practices, including human sacrifices and cutting and exposing the heads off their enemies.

All this was handled by a cast of learned priests, the Druids, who dealt with such sacrifices as well as with law and justice, the keeping of knowledge and traditions in all kinds of religious matters, the cosmos, calendar and divination. Perceived by the Romans as a counterpower, the Druids were quickly eliminated in Britain (in Ireland where they survived, the Church terminated their function), a destiny that was not shared by their religion. Celtic religious beliefs belonged to a shared Indo-European background and, despite important differences, would not be perceived as totally alien by Romans. In fact Romans, with their need for natural representation, gave for the first time a face to many Celtic gods and, by assimilating them with Roman ones, created a new Romano-Celtic religion.

In Britain the new religion included the transformation and assimilation of both traditional Roman and Celtic gods. Among the Roman gods, Mars, the god of war, and Mercury, the god of trade, were by far the most popular. These were polymorphic gods, with many attributes and even confused functions on occasions, acceptable to the Celtic mentality. Often represented were Jupiter, the sky god, Hercules and to a lesser extent, Apollo the god of healing and prophecy. Among the goddesses Juno, Minerva, Venus, Fortuna, Victory, Diana and Ceres, a corn goddess, were the most worshipped. Prominent Celtic gods included mother-goddesses, Epona, the horse-goddess, Sucellus, the hammer-god, and Nodens whose major sanctuary was on the river Severn at Lidney, Gloucestershire. Did this 'new' religion ever reach Ireland?

A NEW IRISH PANTHEON

It did. Through war and commerce, Mars and Mercury were probably the first gods to enter the Irish pantheon. At Alnwick Castle in Northumberland, almost 1,000 years old, the second largest inhabited castle in England after Windsor Castle, a small bronze helmeted figure is kept which is said to have been found in County Roscommon, Ireland. The statuette, 'of rude and early workmanship', seems to represent Mars in a way that strongly indicates the impact of a Celtic milieu.[3] In Britain the greater the Celtic influence, the more often Mars is depicted with crude simplicity, as in the case of *Mars Cocidius* from Bewcastle, Cumbria. In this last, as in several other cases from Britain, Mars is identified with Celtic deities, sometimes without any warlike connotation, such as the British god Nodens, Irish Nuada, who will be part of our story later on.[4]

Another statuette, this time from the river Roe in the very north-east of Ireland, represents the god Mercury. It is a figurine of a rare type with wings on hands, feet and head and a raised leg, similar to British examples from Bristol and Perth.[5] One figurine only against more than 60 in Britain. Caesar tell us that the Gauls 'worship Mercury most of all. He has the greatest number of images'. This was evidently not the case in Ireland, but we know that the Celts in general and the Irish in particular were averse to any physical representations of gods, and how this attitude was eventually changed in Britain only by the presence of the Romans there. In Ireland, the situation being substantially different, a major change in attitude may not have occurred, and the cult of the new god may have spread in a somehow invisible way. Archaeological evidence indicates that, in the area surrounding Caugh Hill, where the statuette was found, the Roman influence must have been substantial.

The area is centred around the remains of a fort, situated at the head of the valley of the river Roe not far from Dungiven, County Derry. When the fort was first found in 1935, the discoverers indicated that two Roman coins were excavated just a few miles away. The immediate surrounding area between the River Mourne (in Derry) and the River Bann (in Coleraine), shows a very special concentration of Romano and

Romano-British material. The rivers flow into Lough Foyle, with natural harbouring facilities, a very likely landing place for Roman traders and settlers.

Moving south along the River Mourne, traders and settlers would reach the hillfort of Clogher, County Tyrone, relatively easily, and this access route could explain the presence of sherds of Roman amphorae in a location of otherwise difficult access from the sea. Moving westwards, along the major tributary of the Mourne, the Derg, they would eventually reach Lough Derg, County Donegal, probably since the most ancient times a place of pilgrimage and prayer. Many centuries later thousands of pilgrims from all over Ireland still congregate here during the summer season.

The pilgrims remain three days on a small island, barefoot, with bread and tea as their only food, praying and performing penitential exercises. What their predecessors in ancient times were doing we do not know, but we know that two of them, Ornecnus and Elisa, were Romans or Romanised people, as they left on the island a pre-Christian stone inscribed in Roman capitals, the only Roman inscribed stone in the whole of Ireland. The stone has been subject to all kinds of interpretation in order to extract from its incomplete text a reading that would make it a Christian memorial. In vain. Ornecnus and Elisa are not *orantes* (praying) as the letters OR of the first line could wrongly lead one to believe, but are somehow involved with *somnium*, dream.[6] Were they in Lough Derg for the purpose of obtaining an oracular vision or to worship some deity of water or otherworld? The answer lies perhaps where we started, at the mouth of the River Roe, on the old shore line of Lough Foyle.

Here in 1896, a marvellous golden hoard – the Broighter hoard – was found consisting of a model boat, a bowl, two chain necklaces, two rod-twisted bracelets and a hollow tubular gold collar with repoussé work. The extraordinary discovery began controversy between the British Museum and the Royal Irish Academy, two institutions of the same State at that time, for its custody. The crown itself, in the person of King Edward VII, had to intervene with a final decision that allowed the objects to return to Ireland where they are kept among the gems of the

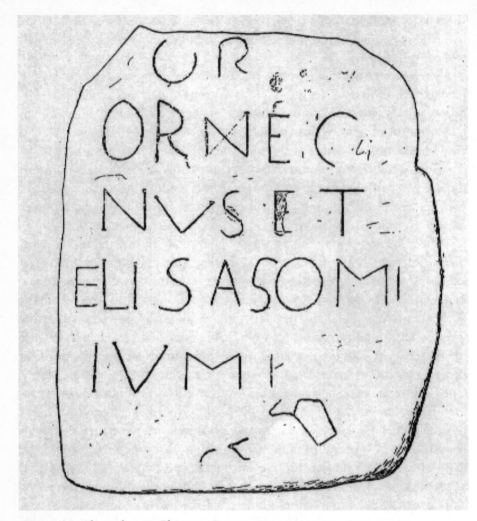

Figure 16. The only pre-Christian Roman inscription on stone.

National Museum. However, troubles were not over because the very origin of some of the objects was insistently questioned with opinions ranging from north-western Europe to as far away as India. Then, in 1982, R.B. Warner produced a complete reappraisal of the hoard with a number of important conclusions relevant for our search of Roman gods in ancient Ireland.

Warner notes that some material is certainly non-native and that the origin of such material, as well as the external influences on the native material, are clearly from the Roman/Mediterranean world. He finds:

> ... that there is more than an associative connection between the Roman and the Irish objects in the Broighter hoard [and suggests] that trade in gold (and perhaps silver) may well be the link between Broighter and the Roman world from, shall we say, the first century AD or earlier.[7]

This connection and link he finds reflected in the decoration of the collar. By a progressive identification of the basic elements in the patterns of the repoussé decoration, Warner manages to highlight two key-elements in the representation, a horse and a hippocamp (sea horse). While the horse is an integral part of Celtic culture, the hippocamp appears to be of classical, Mediterranean inspiration.

Within this Roman-marine inspired context the hypothesis emerges of an undersea or otherworld god, a Celtic Neptunus, that would inhab-

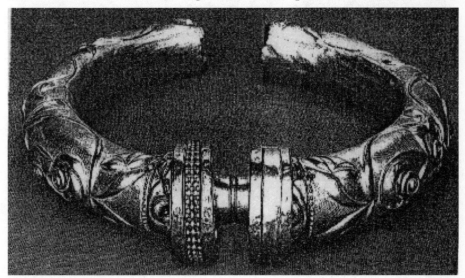

Figure 17. The Broighter gold collar.

141

*Figure 18. Interpreting the decoration (left) of the Broighter Hoard:
(a) a horse; (b) a hippocamp.*

it the waters of Lough Foyle. Warner thinks that this god can be identified in the Irish Manannán:

> ... the popular image of Manannán, the major god of the underworld whose
> undersea realm was apparently entered through Lough Foyle, was hippo-
> morphic, and one would suspect that he was represented artistically in the
> same way.[8]

Did the Celtic cult for Manannán and the Roman cult for Neptunus ever merge in Ireland? There is an Irish water legend that may provide the answer. According to this legend the water-goddess, Boann of the River Boyne, along which, in Newgrange, gold material in many respects similar to that of the Broighter hoard has been found, was associated with the prominent mythological Nechtan. For Warner this association is the missing link:

> I take the association of the Boyne with Nechtan to be an early replacement of Manannán by his classical equivalent Neptunus by Romanised settlers ...[9]

A new Roman god, Neptunus, thus enters Ireland, a god probably worshipped in the Boyne valley, in Lough Foyle and perhaps also by Ornecnus and Elisa in Lough Derg. The new god opens, in turn fascinating insights into the multiform/interchangeable relationship among deities in the Romano-Celtic pantheon. According to an inscription in Chesterholm, Neptunus was identified with Nodens, and we already know that Mars was also identified with Nodens. This last was a very important god in the British pantheon and one that eventually made his way to Ireland under the name of Nuada.

It is difficult to say when this happened, but some clue can be found at his impressive sanctuary in Lidney, Gloucestershire. It was a therapeutic centre, a healing place, as confirmed by a number of dog figurines found there. The dog, whose lapping would treat wounds, was the companion of Aesculapius, the god of medicine. Most importantly, a number of oculist stamps have been found in the sanctuary that immediately remind us of the oculist stamp found in County Tipperary. Could it be that the cult of Nuada as a healing divinity was introduced, or revived, in Ireland during a second Roman invasion in the fourth century AD? The temple in Lidney first built in the third century was extensively refurbished at that time. In the temple Nodens is also represented as a sun-god. What are the implications for Ireland? Let us move to Navan Fort, County Armagh, to disentangle this matter.

NAVAN FORT: JUPITER OR APOLLO?

In 94 BC, according to dendrochronology, a huge quantity of oaks were cut down in the area west of what is now Armagh city, transformed into 275 posts plus a far bigger posthole, and planted in concentric rings to form a 40-metre diameter structure, one of the major monuments in pre-Christian Ireland. Some time, but not much later, the interior of the structure was filled with stones to form a cairn, the external timber wall burned and the cairn covered with a sod mound. It would appear that this impressive building effort and the sequence of events, from its construction to its deliberate destruction within a relatively short period of time, were part of a protracted ritual to a deity, most likely a sun-god, worshipped in that place.[10] But who was this god, was he an indigenous or an imported one, and if imported, what traces did he leave in later Irish sagas and legends?

That Navan was a centre of the cult of some solar divinity seems of little doubt. It suffices to look at the cairn after the removal of the turf mound to see clearly a series of radial divisions on its surface that distinctively hint to a spoked wheel, a very old symbol for the sun in many Indo-European and Celtic cultures that will be integrated into the Roman symbolism and later on into the Christian one. When Jupiter, the Roman sky-god, was introduced in Gaul and Britain, it was assimilated to this solar divinity and also associated with the representation of a wheel.

Evidence has been cited that pre-Roman peoples of non-Mediterranean Europe worshipped a sky-god of their own, probably originating before the Roman and, quite possibly even before the Celtic era. The main sphere of this non-Roman god was that of the sun, hence the consistent symbolism of the spoked wheel ... During the Roman period there appears to have been interaction between the two entities. The physical form of Jupiter appears to have been adopted by the Celts to represent a mixture or fusion between Celtic and Roman divine power; thus the Celtic solar wheel occurs as an attribute alien to the Classical divinity.[11]

If Jupiter is a strong candidate for being the solar divinity worshipped

144

in Navan, another god in the Roman pantheon seems more qualified to be identified as the object of a cult. Apollo was the classical god of youth, prophecy, healing, hunting, music and poetry, a solar god, the second most important god in the Celtic world according to Caesar.

The cult of Apollo travelled a long way. It possibly started in the darkness of early history in Asia Minor, perhaps in Lycia, where an oracle claimed his birthplace to be, and had moved in ancient times to Greece where Apollo became a prominent god, second only to Zeus in the Greek pantheon. By the middle of the first millennium BC, Delphi, the main centre of his cult, had gained a central position among the Greek religious sites. According to the myth, Apollo was born on the small island of Delos, the son of Leto and Zeus. The pregnant Leto, persecuted by the jealous Era, Zeus' wife, had been wandering from land to land, and this was the only refuge she could find to give birth, after nine days of labour pains, to the god and his sister Artemis. By the late sixth and fifth centuries the cult had reached Italy, first Cumae, close to Naples, the venue of the Sibyl, and then Rome. By 433 BC, Apollo had his temple there, by 212 BC, every July the games were organised in his honour. From Rome, and with its conquests, the cult spread practically everywhere. In his Romano-Greek version it was a powerful cult, appealing to people of different cultures, and it is likely to have moved faster than Roman legions in a number of regions. It may have eventually reached Ireland.

The Greek historian Diodorus Siculus, writing in the first century BC, tells us that:

... Hecateus and certain others say that in the regions beyond the land of the Celts there lies in the ocean an island no smaller than Sicily. This island is situated in the north and is inhabited by the Hyperborean ... And there is also in the island a magnificent sacred precinct of Apollo and a notable temple that is adorned with many votive offerings and is spherical in shape ... The myth also relates that certain Greeks visited the Hyperboreans and left behind them there costly-votive offerings ... [12]

Figure 19. The symbol of the spoked wheel in Ireland: Navan fort (top); Celtic representation (middle); christian representation (bottom).

Could this sacred precinct be identified with Navan fort? It could, according to R.B Wagner, making the case for Navan fort with great authority and interesting arguments. The first argument is the *spherical shape* mentioned by Diodorus. Navan is a circular building and so are many examples of Apollo temples elsewhere. In Britain the shrine of Apollo at Nettleton has radiating walls which resemble the concentric organisation of the Navan's posts. Intriguingly, we find a similar radial organisation in the fifth-century church of San Stefano Rotondo in Rome.

The second argument is the fact that, according to Diodorus, the temple to Apollo was *in use* at his time, and so was Navan fort but not other competitors for this attribution, such as Stonehenge. The third argument is an *ape skull* from North-Africa found in Navan confirming the links with the Mediterranean world, perhaps one of the gifts of the visitors from Delos? The fourth argument is a significant coincidence, between the intentional *burning* of Navan fort and the burning, every nine years, at Delphi of a wooden structure especially built for that purpose. Eventually, according to Warner, the cult of Apollo passed into Irish mythology. The comparison between the hero Cú Chullain of the Ulster cycle and Apollo shows an amazing coincidence of essential features.[13]

GREEK MYTHOLOGY	IRISH MYTHOLOGY
Leto bore twins, a boy (Apollo) and a girl (Artemis).	Macha bore twins, a boy and a girl.
Leto suffered appalling labour pains for nine days.	Macha suffered appalling labour pains for 4 days and 5 nights.
Apollo was associated with dogs or wolves.	Cú Chulainn was associated with a dog.
Apollo killed a monster (serpent) as a child and had to atone for it.	Cú Chulainn killed a monster (dog) as a child and had to atone for it.
Apollo's arrows were unstoppable.	The *Gai Bulga* of Cú Chulainn was unstoppable.
Apollo (as Abaris) rode on his arrow in flight.	Cú Chulainn rode on his javelin in flight.

GREEK MYTHOLOGY	IRISH MYTHOLOGY
Apollo made his entry to Delphi with his chariot hitched to swans.	Cú Chulainn made his entry to Emain Macha with swans tied to his chariot.
Apollo was a beardless youth with golden locks.	Cú Chulainn was a beardless youth with golden locks.
Apollo went to the rescue of Troy.	Cú Chulainn went to the rescue of Emain Macha
Apollo was killed in a fight with a water monster.	*Fergus Leite / mac Roich* was killed in a fight with a water monster.

Out of this sea of evidence, suggestions and concomitant hints, R.B. Warner draws a final conclusion:

I am suggesting that there was a god whose influence was widespread over western Europe, who may well have originated in the west but was borrowed by the Greeks and Romans. His attributes included youth, hunting skills, healing, and he was especially associated with the sun. He was, in short, the life-giving god in distinction to the darker gods of the depths. He went by different names in different places, he was Apollo in the Classical world, he probably had a similar but now lost name in his place of origin (which I shall explore at another time) and the Celtic speakers of Gaul and Britain associated him with various local Celtic gods with similar attributes. The myths associated with Apollo were, I suggest, transferred to these local gods and remained with them in their transition into the later legends of Wales and Ireland.

He was the god to whom the Navan enclosure was dedicated and to whom the 40-metre 'temple' was erected and burned. Conmáel mac Ébir was an early double and Cú Chulainn was his later embodiment in the Ulster Cycle tales.[14]

If the cult of Apollo entered Ireland, it is likely that the cult of Hercules also did. The two cults had significant elements of interchangeability. At Aix-les-Bains,in a thermal complex, bronzes of Hercules, instead of Apollo, have been found. At Ambracia, in Greece, after the capture of the town by the Romans in 189 BC, a temple to Hercules and the Muses was erected, while in Rome, in the temple of Apollo, the Muses were represented in a famous statuary group by Filiscus of Rhodes. Both Apollo and Hercules were given the epithet *musagetes*, leader of the Muses.

The Celts must have found this macho semi-god skilled in music and eloquence particularly attractive. In the second century AD the Greek writer Lucian, while visiting Gaul, saw a picture of an old man in a skin leading a group of men who were attached to his tongue by gold and amber chains starting from their ears. It was explained that the picture represented Hercules in his lion skin and symbolised eloquence, a virtue much appreciated by the Celts. Several centuries later we find an almost identical description in the central epic of the Ulster cycle, *Táin Bo Cualnge* (the Cattle-Raid of Cooley) where a dark man is pictured with seven chains around his neck, each one with a head attached at its end. The cult of Hercules could have survived in Irish legend.

On the female side, we can reasonably suspect that Minerva made some entry into the Irish pantheon. We already know that on the other side of the Irish Sea, in Bath, Minerva Sulis was worshipped in a major temple and that this was a centre of cultural, artistic and religious interchange between the Roman and Celtic cultures. Minerva Sulis was, in fact, a combination of the Roman goddess with a pre-existing Celtic goddess of similar attributes. Brighid, the Irish goddess of poetry and knowledge, craftsmanship and healing which we find with the name Briganti as the protector goddess of the powerful British tribe of Brigantes, also had very similar attributes. Some intermingling of the two cults across the Irish Sea seems quite probable, but intermingling among religions must have lasted longer, well into the Christian era since Brighid managed to transform herself into the abbess of Kildare monastery, eventually to become a celebrated saint in the Irish Church. It was not an isolated case. The Celtic god Lug, the equivalent of the Roman Mercury, underwent a series of amazing transformations to appear in different guises: as the great Irish hero of the Fenian Cycle, Finn mac Cumaill, as St Patrick

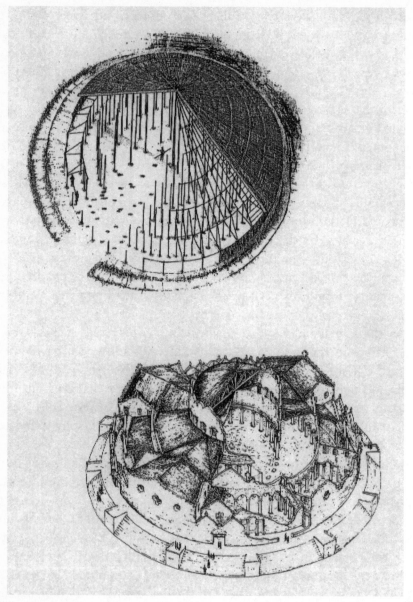

Figure 20. Radial structure in the Navan Fort (top) and in the church of San Stefano Rotondo in Rome (bottom).

himself, even as *leprechaun* (a corrupted version of *Lug-chorpan / Lug-*little body) in modern tales.[15]

Having ventured rather far into the realm of myths and legends, it is time to come back to where all religions start and end, burials and the cult of the dead, and to explore the emerging pattern of crucial changes towards Christianity.

ANTICIPATING CHRISTIANITY

There are a number of burials of the first and second centuries AD that are often dealt with separately in archaeological books on Ireland, since the objects found therein are clearly Roman or with strong Roman influence. It is not easy to place them within the contemporary profile of an Irish burial usually consisting of a pit, cist or mound with little more than a dead body or ashes. They are therefore usually classified as 'intrusive' and treated accordingly.

As we have seen, in *c.* 1850, in 'Loughey' on the County Down coast, near Donaghadee, a burial was discovered containing a hoard of Roman objects of the first century AD. Its contents consisted of several bronze tweezers, two bronze rings, a bronze fibula, the bowl of a spoon, 152 coloured glass beads, an armlet of purple glass, an armlet of shale, brass coins and some other objects less fully recorded. The burial site was destroyed by the finder interested only in the hoard. Some of the objects have also been lost. The others are now dispersed between the British Museum and the Ashmolean Museum in Oxford.

In the same year on the River Nore in Stoneyford, County Kilkenny, the remains of a Roman classical burial were found. At the time of the find, the remains consisted of a plain, light green glass urn with human bones in it, a glass lachrymatory and a bronze circular mirror used as a cover to the urn. Not very far away from these three objects, three more were found: a finger ring and two bronze toilet implements.

Another burial place was discovered in Lambay, a small island off the north Dublin coast. Here, in the early 1840s, a Roman coin was found which has since been lost. A second discovery, some time before the 1860s, involved a decorated gold band and a sword which again is also lost. A third discovery occurred in 1927, when works were undertaken in the island harbour, with many objects found in association with crouched burials. The graves were immediately destroyed by the excavators and the objects passed from hand to hand until reaching the National Museum twenty years after their discovery. When they reached the museum they consisted of a beaded bronze collar, eight rings of various sizes and materials, five bronze *fibulae* or brooches, three bronze scabbard-mounts, many sheet bronze fragments as well as a mirror and an iron sword, which are apparently now missing.

A fourth burial site was unearthed near Bray, County Wicklow, in 1835. On exposure to the air the bones crumbled to dust, while the grave itself, a long stone cist grave with the skeletons lying regularly east to west, was apparently destroyed when building the new railway line a few years later. What remained was a number of Roman copper coins of the second century whose fate is unknown.

The appalling fate of these alien burials is a great shame because they contained objects of extreme archaeological value and signal the introduction of a number of Roman burial customs into Ireland, which changed the way the Irish buried their dead.

The most important is the progressive passage from cremation to inhumation practiced in three of the four burials under consideration. Inhumation and cremation had been coexisting in most places at this time, including in the Mediterranean and Celtic cultures. In Rome, during the Republican period, both rituals were in use with inhumation prevailing in the lower classes for economic reasons and cremation being rather the privilege of the higher strata in society. However, during the empire, under the influence of oriental cults and subsequently Christianity, inhumation progressively became the prevailing form. Both inhumation and cremation had also been practised by the Irish since the earliest times, but with cremation more frequent than inhumation. Now, at the beginning of the first millennium AD, under Roman influence, this ratio is definitively reversed and inhumation progressively becomes the usual way of burying in Ireland.

Other practices, typically Roman, are the laying of the dead in an extended position, the body orientated east to west with the head toward the west, in a long stone cist burial. This is exactly the case in the burial of Bray Head according to records. The crouched burial of Lambay Island also shows an imported practice, possibly from Britain. Eventually the Roman practice prevailed and became general.

The change was not sudden. Different burial practices continued to co-exist well into the Christian period, nor did the introduction of the new Roman customs happen overnight. The four intrusive burials above are only the tip of the iceberg. Romanisation of burying practices developed in time, and the presence of Roman traits progressively infiltrating some of the more 'traditional' burials, seems to confirm it. At Betaghstown and Knowth, County Meath, at Grannagh, County Galway, as well as in a number of other long stone cists scattered throughout the country, signs of Roman presence or influence have been detected. By entering the most secluded and reserved area of burial practice, one in which the cultural identity of people expresses itself unconditionally, Romanisation reached the very heart of Irish civilisation and further paved the way towards the Christianisation of Ireland.

It is recognised here that systemic change is often internal (endogenous) and most of the changes within Early Christian Ireland were generated internally. But there can be no doubt that the very origins of early Christian Ireland itself were external. The significant forces (such as the adoption of Christianity) acting on the Iron Age sociocultural system in the fourth and fifth centuries were from parts of the Romanised world, and led to major irreversible structural changes to the system.[16]

SAINT PATRICK WAS A ROMAN CITIZEN

Carbury Hill, County Kildare, at the source of the Boyne, is in a crucial logistic position. As discussed, this area was possibly associated with the cult of *Nechtan*/Neptunus and its introduction by Roman settlers. We have also noted its proximity to Newgrange where important Roman finds have been made. At Carbury Hill the finds are much less impressive but not less significant for our story. At a burial excavated there in the

1930s, a silver jet spoon with swan's neck handle was found that has clear parallels with late Roman spoons[17] and also close associations with early Christian material, so much so that it has been interpreted as one of the very first pieces of evidence of Christian penetration in Ireland.[18]

Such a small object appears as an emblem of how Christianity might have been introduced into Ireland, an introduction that may not have been the 'big bang' many believe it was but just a privileged moment within a progressive process of assimilation of cultures and practices of life often, and perhaps improperly expressed by the term Romanisation. The spoon of Carbury tells us more about the crucial changes that occurred in Ireland at this time than the many late Medieval heroic histories of religious conquest of the country by Christianity.

Christianity seems to have moved into Ireland in this form already in the fourth century, following moving populations, returning soldiers, slaves, trade, religious practices, new fashion, new technologies and new ideas originating from the Roman world that had slowly penetrated into Ireland and become an integral part of its culture. 'It would have been a process of infiltration, slow and almost imperceptible'.[19] As a result of this process when, according to Prosper of Aquitaine and his *Chronicle*, Palladius was sent to Ireland by Pope Celestine in AD 431, a Christian community must have already been in existence. Palladius was, in fact, a bishop, the first bishop of Ireland, and bishops were not sent to a country to convert the natives but to rule a community of believers.

Where Palladius landed and started his mission is unknown and later sources can only provide some hints. The names of two continental saints, that tradition has as companions of the British Patrick and could, in fact, be disciples of Palladius, he also being a continental, are incorporated in the place-names of Killashee (the cell of Auxonius) County Kildare and Dunshaughlin (the fort of Secundinus) County Meath.[20] Palladius himself is said to have built three churches in County Wicklow, one of which has the significant name of *Tech na Roman*, House of the Romans.[21] Based on these sources and traditions, the eastern part of Ireland, the most Romanised, would have been the centre of Palladius' activity.

Prosper of Aquitaine also tells us that in order to combat the Pelagian heresy, Pope Celestine sent Germanus, Bishop of Auxerre, to Britain, adding that this was done on the instigation of the deacon Palladius. If Palladius, first bishop of Ireland, is the deacon mentioned in the *Chronicle*, as it appears most likely, his familiarity with Rome and Roman things is beyond doubt. In fact, he was probably a member of the local aristocracy, of the élite that had personified the very essence of *Romanitas* during the empire and would continue to do so until its end and beyond.

Patrick should be seen in a similar context. As he himself tells us in his *Confessions,* he was the son of Calpornius, a deacon, and the grandson of Potitus, a priest, two exponents of the Romano-British upper class who were carrying on in public, and to a large extent in private life, the 'Roman way' two decades after the Romans had left the country.[22] Despite the fact that Patrick defines himself as 'most unlearned' in his *Confessions,* he must have had, within such a highly Romanised context, an early classical education, having apparently studied theology under Germanus himself at Auxerre before moving to Ireland. Germanus was a leading figure of the Gallican church and Auxerre one of the most important centres of Romano-Gaulish civilisation. Patrick spoke and wrote Latin, with a British accent, as the Irish would do for many centuries to come.[23] Although the quality of his Latin has been the object of many commentaries, this was his mother tongue. He was a Romano-British and a Roman citizen at birth.

At sixteen Patrick had an adventure that changed his life. He was captured by pirates and taken to Ireland where he spent six years in servitude. Eventually he escaped back to Britain but, having converted to Christianity in the meantime, he refused to continue his previous life and moved to Ireland to evangelise the country. His area of operation was primarily the north-east, and we know that this part of Ireland was under great Roman influence, but places all around the country have traces of his missionary activity, often in previously Romanised contexts. We have already discussed Patrick's presence at Lough Derg where the only Roman classical inscription in the entire country has been found. We have mentioned the unfortunate encounter at Cashel where Patrick stabbed the local king with his crozier, and also the fact that the Cashel area was a most likely destination for a second invasion of Ireland by Roman *foederati* in the fourth century. As a possible follow-up to this invasion it was suggested that Irish populations moved to Wales, a move perhaps reflected in the tradition of the dispossessed tribe of the Desii. In Wales, the Irish settled and became familiar with the Roman culture. They were eventually absorbed in the south and possibly expelled from the north early in the fifth century, according to the traditional story of the defeat of the Irish king of Gwynedd. It has been suggested that a wave of counter-migration could have taken place as a consequence of that defeat with fully Romanised and Christianised Irish returning to Ireland to found the Rock of Cashel and make Cashel a centre of Christianity.[24]

At Tara, where Patrick, according to tradition, appeared during the annual festival called 'Baal's fire' and convinced the local king to embrace Christianity, Roman glass and pottery, a lock, a seal and a very fine set of compasses in bronze, which is definitely of Mediterranean origin, have been discovered. Altogether Patrick was moving within a somehow Romanised milieu and this may explain why, despite all difficulties encountered, he managed to convert, often with surprising results, people apparently alien to his message. It is a story of success, fights and conversions in an epic crescendo that has been identified simply with the start of the Irish Renaissance and loaded later with patriotic significance. A personal story that has been perhaps overemphasised:

> Patrick's story of capture, enslavement, escape and final return to Ireland to proselytise has tended to dominate the nature of missionary activity in Ireland to the exclusion of other, less dramatic, but probably more common processes.[25]

Among these processes perhaps the most significant one was Romanisation, in particular the fact that not only had Romanisation preceded and paved the way for Christianity so that, as N. Edwards notes, '... the introduction of Christianity was a lasting aspect of the Roman impact in Ireland'[26] but also that Romanisation and Christianity developed hand in hand in the early centuries of Irish history.

CELTIC OR ROMAN CHURCH?

In AD 664 at Whitby in Northumbria, a synod took place to decide two issues of great importance: the date of the Easter celebrations and the type of tonsure to be used by monks. Behind these issues was a hidden agenda of even greater importance. Should the customs of the Celtic Church, autonomously developed for more than two centuries in several countries, or those rooted in the traditions of the Roman Church, be followed? King Oswieu, who had the final decision, opted for the second alternative and Ireland conformed to the decision. The Roman Church, despite great differences, was to remain the final reference for the development of the Irish Church. Two stones, one at Whitehorn, in Scotland, the other at Kilnassagart, County Armagh, confirm that this was the case. Both mention Peter the Apostle, the founder of the Roman church, in whose name and veneration King Oswieu apparently made his decision. 'The seal of the lodging of Peter the Apostle', reads the first inscription; 'This place did Ternoc, son of Ciaran the little bequeath under the protection of Peter the Apostle', reads the second, and we can possibly date the personage and the inscription at *c*. AD 715, in the aftermath of the synod of Whitby.[27]

It is now increasingly recognised that the case of the Celtic Church has been over-simplified, as it appears to have been built on idiosyncrasies rather than on substantial issues, and there is no evidence for a pan-Celtic Church or for its independence from Rome.[28]

In reality, during the two centuries elapsing between the arrival of Patrick and the Synod of Whitby, the process of Romanisation had been continuing in Ireland facilitated by the rapid expansion of the Church. Not only had the Roman Church introduced Latin, but Latin terminology had spread into the Irish language, and infiltrated the toponymy of the country with Latin words embedded into the emerging Irish culture.

Place names that up to then had been exclusively Irish, began to be based on Latin words. *Domnach*, church, later anglicised as *Donagh*, was used widely in the country. It comes from the Latin *Dominicum*, possibly a very early introduction, if by the end of the fifth century the word was no longer in use. It was replaced by the Latin word *Cella*, perhaps as a sign of the passage from a more episcopal to a more monastic Church. Killashee, the cell of Auxonius, is one example of place names with the same root.

The Church itself represented a new organisation widely inspired by the Roman imperial model. It was a centralised and hierarchical organisation but also a very flexible and articulated one with the idea and practice of Roman *civitates*, cities, and their administrative jurisdiction playing a major role within the system. In most cases the bishops of the emerging church would have their see in one of these *civitates*, where secular and pastoral matters would be dealt with somehow in parallel if not in combination. With the decline of imperial authority, often followed by a kind of institutional vacuum, the role of the Church in many places became central not only to religious but to civic life in general.

In Ireland, with a lack of pre-existing cities, the model could not be developed in exactly the same way, but the sees of the bishops were named *civitates* and so were the monastic centres that progressively emerged. Although in competition, and some time, in conflict with the 'official' Church on religious practices, these centres were also structured and organised entities that may have facilitated, rather than hindered, the penetration in Ireland of a system based on the idea of *civitas*. Altogether, it was the Church that became the catalyst for the development of a completely new type of human settlement for Ireland, the city, and the new type of social organisation attached to it.

Not only were religious and social organisations changing but also the way such organisations were ruled. It is usually accepted that Classical Roman law, still the backbone of the legal system in all countries with a civil law system as opposed to a common law system, had no direct influence on Irish law. This is certainly true if we look at the mechanics of transferring legal rule from one system to another, but it can be questioned if we look at the systems in a wider perspective. Apart from similarities between the Roman and the Irish systems of law, which may simply be the relics of common Indo-European background, the recourse in Irish law texts to the concept of *recht aicnid* (natural law) could be seen as echoing the concept of *ius naturalis in* Roman jurisprudence.

The Roman system of law also influenced the law of the Irish Church itself, the Canon law. Canon law was different to the Roman law in content, dealing in principle, though often only in principle, with religious rather than secular issues, but it did not differ in concept since it was elaborated by canonists whose only available model of reference was Roman law. In turn Canon law profoundly influenced Irish law. The *Corpus Iuris Hibernici* contains the full collection of all texts, glosses and commentaries of ancient Irish law. The greater part of the material in the *Corpus* is in Irish but there are 135 sentences in Latin, all with sources in Canon law, 'thus indicating a connection between vernacular and Canon law lasting well beyond the Norman invasion'.[29]

Progressively, through the Church, a new concept of property spread in Ireland that had originated in the Roman legal concept of individual property. Common land property, belonging not to the individual but to groups, tribes or families, had been the prominent form of property in ancient Rome and it still was in early medieval times in Ireland. In Rome, however, a new model had emerged, based on the individual ownership of land, *dominium*, that had progressively become widespread throughout the empire. Collective land property never fully disappeared, and the practice is still in existence today as the examples of *alpages* in France and *commons* in Britain clearly indicate. Despite these exceptions the Roman model of individual land ownership eventually became widespread. In turn, the new concept of individual property further enhanced the emergence of concepts of individual autonomy and responsibility leading to new entrepreneurial attitudes and the development of a new economy in Ireland.

> The freeing of the individual from ideological constraints emphasising group obligation was largely through Christianity, but was also inherent in some pagan Roman beliefs too. This meant that optimising strategies could be perceived and carried out on radically different lines. The 'entrepreneur'

could experiment, less encumbered with the conservatism inherent in wider group responsibilities, able to succeed or fail in new ventures. Innovation was open to those who wished to try it; change was ideologically acceptable.[30]

While all this was happening in Ireland, a new interplay was in action with the Roman world. It was the continuation of the interplay that had been going on for centuries with the Roman empire, only that now the empire was not there anymore and the play had become much more direct and immediate. Communication, through the Church, between a Celtic Ireland, already largely Romanised, and a Roman culture still very lively in the aftermath of the empire, became more frequent and intense than ever. Progressively Irish monks moved and settled all around Europe, bringing the novelty of Irish identity but also receiving, and bringing back to Ireland, the culture of a world that was the heir of Rome. Much of this interplay was in the field of visual art.

CHAPTER 8

Irish Art between Nature and Abstraction

THE JANUS HEADS OF BOA ISLAND

Abstraction, as in the *Book of Kells* or other illuminated manuscripts, is the most exclusive feature of Irish art, an art where the figurative elements of animals and people are transformed into pure lines and motifs and reorganised in unique combinations of spirals, scrolls, interlacing, circles and all kinds of innovative motifs. This cannot be found anywhere else and certainly not in the Mediterranean tradition.

This view is certainly to be shared as far as the uniqueness of Irish art is concerned but can and must be challenged when arguments of unjustified separation and isolation are introduced. We have seen the wealth of interrelationships between the Celtic and Roman world, and Ireland in particular. Forgetting all this is as unrealistic as it is to imagine that the close proximity to Ireland of one of the biggest and longest lasting civilisations of all times had little or no bearing on the development of the island. For 400 years the Roman empire was an immense clearing house where cultures were filtered and melted together to generate what would eventually become modern Europe. Imagining Ireland out of this process does not make much sense. Art was no exception.

Beyond the Classical Mediterranean world with its repertory of mature artistic forms and their multivariate expressions, all locally produced early Christian art has to be accepted as no more than secondary. It is derivative, and almost always manifest through local copies of imperfectly perceived, or inadequately transmitted, models. This comment applies not only to north-

161

west Europe, but also to Africa south of the Roman limit and Assouan (that is Nubia and Ethiopia), to Eurasia north and east of the Danube, and to such curiosities as the Nestorians in central Asia. The Christian religion evolved in the more sophisticated parts of the empire. Its symbolic art was not more than one special offshoot of late classical decorative art and symbolic art *latu sensu* ...[1]

With this background in mind, perhaps the best way to tackle the issue is to organise a trip to County Fermanagh, on the north shores of Lough Erne up to Boa Island, to discover the two mysterious Janiform stone figures standing in the ancient churchyard of Caldragh. The figures, difficult to date but possibly of the first century AD, are so called because they have two-sided heads like the Roman god Janus. Whether they represent Janus or not (most likely not) is not a matter of concern here. What is important is how a Roman figurative representation may have reached Ireland and become part of its cultural heritage.

Bi-faced stone figures were not unknown to the Celtic world, as the La Tène examples of Holzerlingen in Germany (sixth-fifth century BC) or of the shrine of Entremont, near Aix-en Provence, France (122-123 BC) clearly show. The links with the Mediterranean world evident in both representations indicate, however, that they were not the product of a 'disconnected' culture, but rather the result of early contacts and mutual influences between La Tène and ancient classical cultures pre-dating the very emergence of Rome. Rome itself draws extensively from such cultures and the first Roman representation of Janus on its earliest currency, the *aes grave,* in the second decade of the third century BC, is paralleled by similar types of currency among many populations in the Italian peninsula.

Centuries later, we find this very image of Janus on a coin of the German tribe of the *Mediomatrici,* from whom the name of the city of Metz derives. The imitation is somehow cruder than the original but the representation is largely the same. By entering the Celtic world, the image of Janus starts a process of progressive transformation that is evident in further coinage of the same tribe. In a later coin of the *Mediomatrici,* the

figure of Janus loses much of its organic structure to become dominated by quasi geometrical patterns. The nose is a line, the eyes an
oblong triangle, the mouth two circles and the
chin a pointed semi-circle, all features that, in
some way, reappear in the Janus statues of Boa
Island.

Roman coin with Janus head

Are these statues the ultimate Irish
response to the Roman naturalistic representation of Janus? It is possible and if so, they
would confirm that a long process of continuous artistic permeability and cross-fertilisation
between the Roman and the Celtic cultures
had been going on for centuries and that eventually the naturalistic impact of this interface
reached Ireland. At least a part of the more
than 30 Irish statues representing human figures, most likely pre-Christian, could be wit-
nessing such an impact. Enhanced contacts
with the Roman empire during the Roman
presence in Britain further facilitated the emergence of naturalistic expression in Irish art, as
objects of fashion and everyday life described
earlier indicate. When the Romans left Britain,
the artistic influence of the Roman world,
rather than disappearing, continued and greatly contributed to the shaping of the splendour
of Irish art in the centuries to come. It did not
come by accident but as the result of centuries
of progressive cultural interchange:

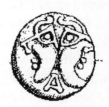

Celtic coin

Celtic coin
derived from previous one

Janus head at Boa island

Some , like the British, had lived mainly within
the Roman provinces; others, such as the Scots
in Ireland and the Picts in Scotland had regular

*Figure 21: Janus heads
from Rome to Ireland.*

163

contact through trading and raiding ... The influence of Roman culture on their lives was profound, if unquantifiable; it is very clear however, that they seized upon certain Roman concepts with enthusiasm and imagination, reinventing them in their own terms and for their own, sometimes very different, purposes.[2]

THE FILIGREE BIRD OF GARRYDUFF

Motifs, symbols, patterns and animal representations borrowed from the Roman world were freshly re-used in Irish art of the fifth, sixth and seven centuries, to be eventually re-absorbed, from the eighth century onwards, into the masterpieces of the Golden Age of such art. New types of ornamental objects, such as belt buckles derived from the Roman military equipment or finger rings of a D-shaped cross section, largely inspired in shape and decoration from Roman models, entered the Irish scene. Finally, new techniques of decoration, millefiori and filigree, that had originated or had been widely diffused in the Roman world, were introduced, which would greatly influence Irish art.

Millefiori was a Roman invention. It involved preparing thin rods of glass of different colours and fusing them together into a single rod. The rod was then cut in slices and the slices placed into a sea of enamel to produce a sensational effect, like a display of 1,000 flowers, *millefiori*. It did not become fashionable in Ireland until the sixth century AD but could have been introduced earlier, in the late fourth or early fifth centuries,[3] possibly directly from the Continent rather than from Britain, since the evidence of millefiori there, apart from some hanging bowls whose provenance, as we will see, is much disputed, is very limited. On the Continent production had started probably in the first or second centuries AD and concentrated primarily in Belgium in the Namur region. In a Roman villa near Dinant, objects with millefiori enamel were produced that were exported as far as southern Russia, Syria and North Africa.[4]

The villa was destroyed by Franks in the third century and the technique became very obscure so that, again, no connection between the Irish production and the Roman one has been suggested. It is enough, however, to compare a buckle-plate found at Lagore, with its two vertical bands of millefiori and a Romano-British buckle-plate found at the South Shield fort, the Roman *Arbeia*, to observe an astonishing similarity in size, shape and decoration, confirming an unequivocal Roman origin of the objects and of the technique. In Ireland the technique was due to become one of the main features of Irish art. The Irish were masters in enamelling and had practised it since the La Tène period, but the introduction of millefiori triggered their fantasy and they quickly introduced this new technique into their production of hand-pins, latchets and penannular brooches. The result was amazing. The plain dress fasteners of the early period gave way to a new production characterised by artistic variety, inventiveness and creativity. At Ballinderry Crannóg 2, a penannular brooch of the seventh century has come to light that clearly shows the impact of this new technique and the not infrequent combination of classical and Celtic styles in one object. Here the millefiori glass is inserted in a red enamel of La Tène inspiration both on the pinhead and the two terminals. The material is poor copper alloy but the manner in which it is textured, a mixture of criss-cross and herringbone patterns, gives the object a silver-like appearance. The overall effect is dramatic and further enhanced by the zoomorphic form of the terminals and the recourse, on their reverse sides, to marigold motifs of clear Roman derivation.

Filigree, twisted gold or silver wire, was another widespread technique with an even longer history in antiquity. It had splendid antecedents in the artwork of the Egyptians, Greeks and Etruscans and was used in Roman jewellery, though with less spectacular results. Starting from the third century AD the Romans revamped the technique with the production of ornamental objects of much higher quality which in turn influenced native production on the Continent. Was the introduction of filigree in Ireland the ultimate result of such developments? Most likely so. Recurrent motifs in Celtic filigree, such as S-scrolls, C-scrolls, spiralling, triskelions and also the use of round wires, twined wires and granulation, often considered exclusive Celtic features, are all techniques rooted in antiquity. Far from being exclusive they are also to be found in Anglo-Saxon art, the most likely medium for these techniques moving from the Continent to Britain and Ireland, as well as in

Byzantine, Merovingian and Lombardic jewellery. This does not necessarily mean direct influence of the filigree from these areas on Irish filigree but seems rather to confirm the common derivation from original
Mediterranean/Roman sources. As pointed out by N. Whitfield: 'In fact
certain resemblances may simply be due to the existence of a common
heritage derived from antiquity.'[5]

By the seventh century AD the technique had reached Ireland and was
well developed. At Lagore a gold filigree ornament was found which
belongs to the building phase of the crannóg, while at Garryduff a filigree
bird was discovered that must have been dropped on and trampled into
the ground at or before the occupation of the site. In both cases there is
a possible dating of around AD 650. The monuments are characterised
by the presence of sub-Roman material or of material of Roman inspiration, particularly relevant in Lagore, but also significant in Garryduff
where 85 sherds, parts of some fifteen vessels of kitchenware, the E ware
mentioned earlier, were found. While Roman influence is evident, it had,
by this time, become part of an amalgam where ultimately, La Tène,
Christian and Germanic elements were all converged into the new emerging forms of Irish art. It is a unique process in Europe.

Finally to sum up, Lagore, like Ireland generally, presents a contrast to the
rest of Europe. In the western Continent a sequence of cultures, Iron Age,
Roman and Germanic, obliterated in turn a considerable part of what had
gone before. In lowland Britain each of these represented an invasion which
spent its force against the British Highland Zone. Elements from each
reached Ireland, but not in sufficient force to blot out what was already
there already. Rather each was absorbed by the existing culture making the
strange combination of Celtic, Roman, Christian and Germanic elements
that characterised the fortress of these Irish kings of the early Middle Ages.[6]

This process of cross-fertilisation was further enhanced by the fact
that Christian and Germanic art had been largely drawn from the
Roman repertoire and that ancient Mediterranean and early La Tène
cultures had intermingled, leaving a trace of shared cultural background

Figure 22. Filigree Garryduff bird (top) and Lagore gold ornament (bottom).

in the manifestations of Roman and Celtic art for many centuries to come. The case of hanging bowls is a good example of how difficult it is to disentangle this matter.

THE ENIGMA OF HANGING BOWLS

The enigma had been there for a long time until, in 1936, Françoise Henry considered the obscure phenomenon of hanging bowls with a revolutionary interpretation which was to generate endless debates for decades to come.

At that time, a little more than 40 of these metal vessels had been discovered, spread over a period of more than half a millennium, (AD 400-900). The bowls were made to be suspended by chains from hooks inserted in escutcheons placed just under their in-turned rim. Their derivation, from late Roman vessels, already was, and still is, unquestioned. Four years before the presentation of Henry's interpretation in the *Journal of Royal Society of the Antiquaries of Ireland,*[7] T.D. Kendrick had shown, in *Antiquity,*[8] the close correlations between hanging bowls and fourth and fifth-century Roman vessels found in Britain, as exemplified by four bowls, part of the Irchester hoard. Further discoveries make clear that the Irchester-type bowl was widely distributed throughout the whole of Britain, and strongly reinforced the importance of the Roman derivation of hanging bowls. This is also clearly reflected in the recurrent use of ornamental motifs of clear Roman origin, such as peltra and trumpet patterns. Even the ascertained fact that the escutcheons were moved from bowl to bowl and sometimes kept as single objects has been seen as confirming this connection.

They may have become regarded as symbols of Romanitas and possibly were used as gift exchange for status building in Anglo-Saxon England.[9]

Apart from this, little else was known except that most hanging bowls had been found in seventh-century Anglo-Saxon graves, without this meaning in any way that they were contemporary to such graves. They had been produced, it was argued, in Britain, raided by the new conquerors and eventually buried with them in later times. But no work-shop for their production has yet been discovered, nor have they been found in contexts that could clarify exactly what they were used for. Altogether they were a mystery.

Henry unsettled even the little that was known. She did not question the Roman origin of hanging bowls but strongly rejected an exclusive British provenance for these vessels. At least part of them, all those enam-elled, she argued, were of Irish origin. To understand how bold this state-ment was, one must know that not one single hanging bowl has ever been found in Ireland and that two escutcheons, one most likely to be an import from Scotland, are the only meagre evidence available. It would have discouraged anyone else. It did not discourage Françoise Henry.

She built up her case using both stylistic and technique-based argu-ments, an area that, at the age of 34, she had completely mastered and in which she was due to become an indisputable authority. It was impossi-ble, she argued, that monochrome-red, enamelled hanging bowls could have been made in Britain because original red enamelling had become fully polychrome there by the end of the first century AD. It would be unreasonable to imagine a reversing of taste, centuries later, just for this type of object. On the other hand, similarities in decoration with other enamelled Irish objects, such as penannular brooches, latchets and pins were so evident as to make their Irish origin unquestionable. The history of these vessels could then be re-written.

If they were lamps used in British churches, their introduction into Ireland would go back to the time of St Patrick. In the first half of the fifth century there were churches in Roman Britain and the effect of the Saxon invasion had not yet begun to be felt. It would be only normal that the newly-found-ed churches in Ireland should have got their ecclesiastical furniture from the nearest point which could supply it. Once the type was introduced into Ireland it would be copied there, with, normally enough, an addition of enamel, after the fashion of the Irish metalwork. Then the advance of the Saxons in Britain must have put a stop to the British fabrication but the hanging bowl would have continued to develop, along new lines, in Ireland

and would probably have been supplied, from there, to the surviving British churches, where the Saxons, advancing still further, would have found them, ripped them from their chains, and treasured them until, as precious property, they would have been buried with their plunders. It then becomes clear why no examples have been found in Ireland: it is normal enough that pins and brooches, dropping by chance from the clothes they were fastening, should be preserved in the ground for future excavators, but the lamps are hardly likely to be lost in the same way.[10]

More than 70 years later, with the number of finds almost doubled, this interpretation is strongly challenged. Despite the numerous discoveries of hanging bowls, their presence in Ireland has still to be shown and the only workshop for their production found in the meantime is located at Craig Phadrig in Inverness! The real use of the bowls is still largely unexplained and the one-way stylistic reading of Henry is largely rejected.[11] It is increasingly clear how an approach opposing British, Irish, Pict and Anglo-Saxon traditions cannot provide an appropriate understanding of an artistic phenomenon that is the result of mutual enrichment, hybridisation and cross-fertilisation. Within this context the Roman tradition plays a major role. Not only do hanging bowls originate from Roman vessels, have ornamental motifs of typical Roman inspiration and adopt the *millefiori* technique borrowed from the Roman world, but they are also an important entry point for Mediterranean naturalistic elements into the flourishing Irish Christian art. Let us take the case of the Benty Grange escutcheon, found in Derbyshire, and its fantastic beasts.

The three creatures shown on the escutcheon are not fantastic at all, rather they represent a stylised representation of the classical Mediterranean motif of dolphins. It is not the only case. We find two dolphins and a cross on the escutcheon of a hanging bowl found at Faversham, Kent, and two dolphins and a ball, a typically classical arrangement, on an Irish ringhead pin from Armoy, County Antrim. In antiquity dolphins were attributes of Neptune, the sea-god and of Venus, born from the sea. Bacchus, kidnapped by pirates, transformed them into dolphins, Fortuna (Chance) was represented as riding dolphins and the

Figure 23. The motif of dolphins from Roman to Irish Art: mosaic from Carthage, Tunisia (top); escutcheon from Benty Grange, Derbyshire (middle); Book of Durrow (bottom) .

coach of the Nereid Galatea was pulled by dolphins. In the early Christian world the fish was often a dolphin symbolising the death and resurrection of Christ. The dolphins of Benty Grange are a further expression of this long tradition.

A mosaic panel from fourth-century Carthage, in Tunisia, shows a motif similar to that of Benty Grange and the same motif, even further stylised, can be found in the Book of Durrow, the earliest of the great illuminated manuscripts. It has been suggested that Germanic art could rather be the source of inspiration of the book of Durrow's animals but it would not make a great difference for the sake of our argument. When the Roman empire collapsed, zoomorphic patterns, like the one of dolphins, were integrated into the art of the German peoples. A dolphin representation, not unlike the one at Bentry Grange, can be found on a German metal disc from Wehde. However, artistic inspiration appears in the Book of Durrow of a more naturalistic type than in the disc from Wehde and closer to that shown in the dolphin of Bentry Grange. It has been concluded that: '... it seems possible to assume that the Durrow animals are derived ultimately from Mediterranean models with a certain influence from Germanic style II.'[12]

STAGS AND GRIFFONS IN THE DERRYNAFLAN HOARD

When Christianity eventually entered Ireland, naturalistic elements borrowed from the Roman tradition continued to develop into the art of illuminated manuscripts, high crosses and metalwork, well into the Middle Ages. Two recently discovered eighth-ninth century hoards show how this influence manifested itself concretely. The case of hoards is of particular interest, these being primarily constituted of portable objects, themselves a natural vehicle for the spreading of stylistic features.

In autumn 1984, during drainage works on the banks of the river Moynalty near the townland of Donore, County Meath, a hoard came to light composed essentially of two tinned-bronze hammered discs, a tinned-bronze plaque and an assembly composed of a circular frame, an animal-head handle and a ring. The head is that of a lion of striking naturalism, a motif with many antecedents in classical antiquity and recurrent in Roman handles with funerary or sacral functions.

A few years before, another hoard had been discovered in County Tipperary, the Derrynaflan hoard, after the name of the ancient monastery where it was found. Like the Donore hoard, the Derrynaflan is capable of competing in refinery and splendour with the great masterpieces of Irish art such as the Ardagh chalice or the Tara Brooch. It consists of five objects: a paten, a stand for the paten, a chalice, a strainer and a much-worn basin.

Both the paten and the chalice are inspired by late Roman tableware, and some of the iconographical models in the chalice and the paten are of Roman origin. This last contains 24 filigree panels with abstract representations. It is, however, enough to look more attentively within the interlaced motifs of some of the panels to discover animals and human figures of naturalistic inspiration, such as a stag with snakes, an eagle with a two-headed snake, and a pair of men. The animals and the related symbolism have their antecedents in the Roman world. It is more difficult to trace the ancestry in the case of the two men, but as Michael Ryan, a leading expert in early Irish metalwork points out: 'These [two men] ... signal the remote ancestry of the paten in late-antique tableware and reflect the preservation and use in contemporary western European church treasuries of late Roman-style plate with rim ornament of manikins and beasts.'[13]

The chalice also contains animal representations. Of its 84 filigree panels, 47 are zoomorphic and 37 show complete animals. Around fifteen of these are birds, possibly griffons, of clear Mediterranean inspiration and, though represented in a more abstract way than in the case of the paten, they confirm the persistence of a clearly detectable classical vein in the Irish metalwork, many centuries after the collapse of the Roman empire. Not everything, of course, was of Roman origin. Many motifs were of Anglo-Saxon, Germanic and Christian inspiration. Oriental sources of inspiration have also been strongly proposed based on some stylistic similarities between Irish chalices and chalices from Syria or Byzantium.

The idea that significant elements in early Irish Christian art could be

Figure 24. Stag (top) and eagle (bottom) from Derrynaflan paten.

derived from Coptic Egypt, Syria or Armenia has been repeatedly put forward to become eventually a quite popular opinion. Artistic influence from these regions would also be responsible for the 'carpet' (fully ornate) page, interlace and dot-contouring in Irish illuminated manuscripts, as well as for some similarities between cross slabs and high cross representations in Christian Egypt and Ireland. The medium would have been travelling monks from the two sides, as exemplified by the visit of Cummian's delegates to Rome, meeting 'an Egyptian' in the seventh century and the fact that seven Egyptian monks, as told in *Félire Oenguso,* were buried in Ireland at the end of the eighth century. This does not make a very strong case for an oriental connection. The proposers of this idea seem to forget that Egypt was just part of the empire and that the Roman impact on its artistic expression had been important there both before and long after the arrival of Christianity. They also seem to forget that dotting had been present in Irish ornaments well before early Christian times[14] and that, as we will see, interlace and the carpet page could have been inspired by late Roman mosaics. Indirect influences from the Orient to Ireland are not to be excluded, but it is increasingly recognised that, whatever such influences, these originated from a highly Romanised, by now Christian, background and introduced into Ireland through Rome.

Equally clear, when Christianity came to be organised here under the direction of a mission from Rome led by a Romanised Briton who was trained in Roman Gaul, new ideas, new designs, new subjects came to be added to the repertoire of native art. And there can be little doubt that it was the Roman world which contributed vastly, but not exclusively, to the new development.[15]

THE ROBE OF THE SAINT IS A ROMAN MOSAIC

Centuries before the Donore and Derrynaflan hoards, another hoard had been buried in the townland of Ballinrees, a few miles from Coleraine, County Derry, that well exemplifies the introduction into Ireland of a completely different type of stylistic influence from the Roman world.

We already know that the Coleraine hoard mentioned earlier is the major assemblage of Roman coins in Ireland and we can argue, on the basis of such coins, a dating at the beginning of the fifth century AD. But the Coleraine hoard also contains a series of fragments of silver plate for which, thanks to the contextual presence of the coins, a fairly close dating can also be given, a relatively rare case in the history of art. These fragments present a number of motifs and decorations of a non-naturalistic type, even if some had their original inspiration in nature, that were characteristic of Roman metalwork, but also textile and mosaic Roman art throughout the entire empire. We are no longer dealing only with animal or human figures but with relatively abstract representations,

Figure 25. Ornamental fragments from Coleraine hoard.

which will have significant and long-lasting reflections in later Irish art.

It is true that simple compass-pattern design such as the rosette and the quadrefoil pattern, which were already of great antiquity, survived in the Celts lands for a long time after the Roman period, particularly in Ireland where they remained in use until at least the eighth century.[16]

In the long process of the emergence of new abstract models within Roman art and the spreading of such models beyond the borders of the empire, the Coleraine hoard represents perhaps a minor event but a significant one as far as Ireland is concerned. It helps to break the artificially-established dichotomy between nature and abstraction, and also the artificial link of Roman art with the first form of artistic expression, and of Irish art with the second one. We have seen how the naturalistic influence of Roman art manifested itself in the statues of Boa Island, in the escutcheons of the hanging bowls, in the filigree ornaments of Garryduff and Lagore, and in the paten and chalice of Derrynaflan. Of no less importance is the influence of abstract elements from Roman art on Irish art, and the close interrelationship between these two types of influences, as exemplified by a Roman mosaic discovered in 1793 in the south-west of Britain.

The pride of the village of Woodchester near Stroud, the fourth-century mosaic, the 'great pavement' of a magnificent Roman villa, the biggest north of the Alps, and a masterpiece of its type, lies invisible beneath the floor of the local churchyard. The last time it was opened to public view in 1973, 140,000 visitors invaded the village causing many problems, that it has not been reopened since. The mosaic represents Orpheus surrounded by a dog, tigers, a leopard, an elephant, a boar, birds and fishes organised in two concentric circles around it. But what interests us primarily is the large surrounding area full of decorative elements, including running scrolls, swastikas, meander patterns and concentric circle patterns which are also an integral part of the stylistic patrimony of Celtic design.

In the fourth century AD the art of mosaic underwent a major revival all round the empire and Britain was not an exception. Four main schools were in operation there, the Petuarian at Brough-on-Humber on the north-west coast, the Durobrivan at Chesterton, the Durnovarian at Dorchester and the Corinian at Cirencester. Not a single piece of mosaic has ever been discovered in Ireland but this proximity is important, especially if stylistic similarities are to be found. Why look as far afield as Egypt for possible resemblances when on the other side of the Irish Sea one of the major expressions of Roman art was in full development, and motifs and patterns that would become common in Irish art were not only at hand but could be easily transferred to Ireland by means of portable objects as those, for instance, of the Coleraine hoard? Certainly there is a time lag between the last Roman mosaics in Britain, at the very end of the fourth century, and the first Irish illuminated manuscripts at the end of the sixth and the beginning of the seventh centuries AD. However, the presence of the Roman mosaics in Britain was so widespread (over 1,500 have been discovered up to now, a fraction evidently of the entire production) that their visibility must have been important long after the Romans left the country.

Since the decline of painting starting from the second century AD, mosaics had progressively emerged as a main, if not the major, form of visual art in the Roman empire. This process was accompanied by a progressive sophistication in the presentation of abstract elements and, especially during the fourth-century revival, by a new emphasis on dynamic, rotating elements that greatly increased the liveliness of the design and made it a much more likely source of inspiration for Irish art than the rather rigid and fixed decorations of previous Roman artwork. The same can be said for the variety of colours and shades. The limestone pieces of the Woodchester mosaic present a range of seven different colours and fourteen shades.

But it is not only a matter of decoration. The entire conception of the carpet page in illuminated manuscripts could well reflect the global filling of space in late Roman mosaics. This celebrated innovation of the Book of Durrow appears much more likely to have originated from the total coverage of the surface as it appears, for instance, in the

Woodchester mosaic just a few hundred miles away, rather than in some improbable oriental carpet, produced thousands of miles away in a completely different cultural setting. Interlacing could also have a similar origin as clearly shown by interlaced patterns both in the mosaic of the great pavement and in another mosaic found in the gallery at the Roman villa of Woodchester.

At the time of awakening antiquarian interest in the ancient culture of Ireland, in the middle of the nineteenth century, collections of objects and manuscripts held in the Royal Irish Academy were studied and published. The ornament of this metalwork and these manuscripts inspired a new art which was perceived, somewhat inaccurately, as representative of a Celtic identity and the ribbon interlace and intricate knot patterns remained synonymous with Celtic art ever since ...

Ribbon interlace, although used earlier, sprang from an ornament based on geometrical constructions in Roman mosaics, and continued to have architectural application in the early church. It was therefore ideally suited to the discipline of the grids of the manuscript pages.[17]

That is not all. The impact of Roman heritage on Irish illuminated manuscripts went well beyond abstract representation. It involved, as we have seen, the introduction of a new animal presence that the Irish artists genially developed into zoomorphic interlacing. Human figures, inspired by the Roman-Christian tradition, eventually also entered their repertoire. In the Book of Durrow, the robe of St Matthew seems to come straight from a Romano-British mosaic. Even the script of the manuscripts is a beautifully decorated Roman half-uncial which remained their script up to the tenth and eleventh centuries, defying the introduction and spread throughout the entire west of the Carolingian script. Finally, the evangelist portraits and symbols are clearly borrowed from the late antique tradition, revamping the memories of a classical world long gone. The same world that we find in the scene of a centaur on the west side of a carved pillar at Tibberaghny, County Kilkenny, or in that of a hunter with a spear, inspired by the classical theme of Hippolytus hunting, on the north face of the Bealin Cross, County Westmeath. But manuscripts and crosses are taking us well into the eighth and ninth centuries, far beyond the time frame that we have given to our story. The Roman empire had disappeared four centuries before, and, although the Church and Byzantium and the Carolingian empire were perpetuating in time the Roman model, all this was re-shaped into new realities and, as far as Ireland is concerned, into a largely self-generated, unique development.

CONCLUSION

It has been a long voyage, and I have not provided the answers to all the questions. We know, however, for sure that Ireland and Rome were not two separate worlds and that instead, cultural, artistic, military, commercial, religious and everyday life interplay went on for centuries and greatly contributed to shape the very national identity of the country. It is a very special identity but it did not emerge from nothing or from the twilight of a Celtic world invented by the romantics and the patriots of the nineteenth century. It emerged from Irish people meeting other people from all parts of an immense conglomeration of countries gathered together under the name of Rome and exchanging with them ideas and slaves, personal ornaments and arms, dogs and wine, language and gods and the way of building their houses, and burying their dead and making a water mill or a plough or decorating a bowl or a brooch or using new plants for cultivation. How all this concretely happened is still largely to be discovered and some may wish to continue searching into the unexplored. If Ireland is not a virgin, she is still a wonderful, mysterious lady.

References

CHAPTER 1

1. P. Hunter Blair, *Roman Britain and Early England, 55BC-AD 871*, Thomas Nelson and Sons, Edinburgh, 1963, p. 53.
2. Tacitus, *Agricola*, 24.
3. E. Gibbons, *The History of the Decline and fall of the Roman Empire*, Harper and Brothers Publishers, New York, 1880, Volume I, p. 219.
4. T. J. Sheehy, *Ireland*, Colour Library Books, Godalming, Surrey, England, 1988, p. 24.1988, p. 24
5. Strabo, *Geography*, Book IV.
6. R. K. McElderry, 'Juvenal in Ireland?', *Classical Quarterly*, 37 (1922), p. 151.
7. From a report of V.E. Nash-Williams, National Museum of Wales (where the vessel is kept) which appeared in S.P. Ó Riordáin, 'Roman Material in Ireland', in *PRIA*, Vol. LI, Sec. C, Dublin, 1947, p.65.
8. C. Jullian, *Histoire de la Gaulle*, Vol. II, Paris 1908, 13 No. 5.
9. Polybus, *History*, 2.30.
10. Tacitus, *ibid*.
11. Tacitus, *ibid*, 24.
12. *Classical Review*, 11, 1897, p. 328.
13. *Proceedings of the American Philological Association*, July 1899, Vol. XXIX, pp. XXXVI-IX.
14. A. Gudeman, *Tacitus De Vita Julii Agricolae* and *De Germania*, revised edition, Allyn and Bacon, Boston, New York, Chicago, Atlanta, San Francisco, Dallas, 1928, iii.
15. S. Frere, *Britannia*, London, 1978 ed., Routledge and Kegan Paul Ltd., p.135
16. S. Young, *The Work of Angels, Masterpieces of Celtic Metalwork, 6th-9th centuries AD*, British Museum Publications, 1989, London.
17. M.J. O'Kelly, *Early Ireland*, Cambridge University Press, Cambridge, 1995,

p. 265.

18. F. Haverfield, 'Ancient Rome and Ireland', *The English Historical Review*, No. CIX, January 1913, p. 9.

19. E.M. Jope and B.S.C. Wilson, 'A Burial Group of the First Century AD from Loughey, near Donaghadee, County Down', *UJA*, XX, 1957, p.74.

20. J. D. Bateson, 'Roman Material From Ireland: A Re-consideration', in *PRIA*, Vol. LXXIII, Sec. C, 1973, p. 83.

21. J. Carruthers, 'On Roman Remains found in Ireland', *JRSAI*, 1856, IV, p. 164.

22. H. Hencken, 'Lagore Crannóg: An Irish Royal Residence of the 7th to 10th Centuries AD', *PRIA* Vol. LIII, 1950, p. 15.

23. J.D. Bateson, *op. cit.*

24. S. Frere, *Britannia, op. cit,*. pp. 342-343.

25. C.G. Starr, 'The Roman Imperial Navy, 31 BC-AD 324, New York', 1941, 165, No. 105, cited in V.E. Nash-Williams, *The Roman Frontier in Wales*, Cardiff, University of Wales Press, 1969, p. 36.

26. F. Haverfield, 'Ancient Rome in Ireland', in *The English Historical Review*, Vol. XXVIII, 1913, p. 1.

27. S.P. Ó Riordáin, 'Roman Material in Ireland' in *PRIA*. Vol. LI, Sec. C, 1947, p. 35.

28. J.D. Bateson, *op. cit.*, p. 21. See also J.D. Bateson, 'Further finds of Roman material in Ireland', in *PRIA*, Colloquium on Hiberno-Roman Relations and Material Remains (September 1974), Vol. LXXVI, Sec. C, 1976, p. 171.

29. R.B. Warner, 'Tuathal Techmar: A Myth or Ancient Literary Evidence for a Roman Invasion?' in *Emania*, No. 13, 1995, p. 23.

30. R.A.S. Macalister, 'On some antiquities discovered upon Lambay', *PRIA*, 38, Sec. C, 1929, p. 240.

31. E. Rynne, 'The La Tène and Roman Finds from Lambay, County Dublin: A Re-Assessment', in: *PRIA, op. cit.*, Vol. 76, Sec. C, Dublin, 1976, p. 231.

32. J. Maas, 'Roman invasion sparks conflict', *The Sunday Times* (Irish), 28 January 1996.

33. G. Cooney, 'Ireland, the Romans and All That', *Archaeology Ireland*, No. 35 Vol. 10, No. 1, spring 1996, p. 18.

34. B. Raftery, 'Drumanagh and Roman Ireland', *Archaeology Ireland*, No. 35, *op. cit*, p. 18. .

35. 'Letter to the Romans, John Maas Replies', *Archaeology Ireland*, No. 36,

Vol.10, No. 2, Summer 1996, p. 38.

36. R. Warner, 'De Bello Hibernico, A less than edifying debate', *Archaeology Ireland*, No. 37, Autumn 1996, p. 39.

37. C. Adams, 'Hibernia Romana? Ireland and the Roman Empire', *History Ireland*, Summer 1996, p. 22.

38. T. Condit, 'Enigma Delenda Est', *ARA*, Autumn 1996, p. 9.

39. S. Pogatchnick, 'Experts Claim Romans May have Established Colonies in Ireland', *Los Angeles Times*, 17 November 1997, Part A, p.37, retrieved from Electric library 1.10.1997.

40. B. Raftery, *op. cit.*, p.19.

41. J.P. Bushe-Fox, *Fourth Report on the Excavations of the Roman fort at Richborough, De Bello Hibernico, Kent*, The Society of Antiquaries of London, Oxford, 1949, p. 4.

CHAPTER 2

1. F. Henry, 'Remains of the Early Christian Period on Inishkea North, County Mayo', in *Studies in Early Christian and Medieval Irish Art, Vol. III. Architecture and Sculpture*, The Pindar Press, London 1985, p. 203.

2. F. Henry, 'A Wooden Hut on Inishkea North, County Mayo', *op. cit.*, p.273.

3. Pliny, *Historia naturalis*, IV.

4. H.F. McClintock, *Old Irish and Highland Dress*, Dundalk,1950, p. 14.

5. L. and J. Laing, *Celtic Britain and Ireland, The Myth of the Dark Ages*, Irish Academic Press, Worcester, 1990, pp. 178-179.

6. H. Hencken, *op. cit.*, p. 12.

7. H. Hencken, *op. cit.*, p. 16.

8. M. O'Kelly, 'The Two ring Forts at Garryduff, County Cork', *PRIA*, Vol 63, Sec.C, pp 38-39.

9. S. James, *The Atlantic Celts*, British Museum Press, 1999, p. 53.

10. L. and J. Laing, *op. cit.*, p.208.

11. H.E. Kilbride-Jones, 'Zoomorphic Penannular Brooches', *Reports of the Research Committee of the Society of Antiquaries of London*, 1980, p. 135.

12. C. Thomas, 'A Provisional List of Imported Pottery in Post-Roman Western Britain and Ireland', *Institute of Cornish Studies*, 1981, p.23.

13. L. and J. Laing, *op. cit,*. p.159.

14. H. Hencken, *op. cit.*, p. 194.

15. B. Raftery, *Pagan Celtic Ireland*, London,1994, p.141.

16. S.P. Ó Riodáin, *op. cit.*, p. 56.
17. E. Flower, 'The origins and development of the Penannular Brooch in Europe', *Proceeding of the Prehistoric Society*, XXVI (1960), 149-177.
18. L. and J. Laing, *op. cit.*, p. 166.
19. H.E. Kilbride-Jones, 'The evolution of pennanular brooches with zoomor phic terminals in Great Britain and Ireland', in *PRIA* XLIII,C, 1937, 379 ff.
20. Ó Riordáin, *op. cit,*. p. 35.
21. J. Raftery, 'Bronze Zoomorphic Brooch from Toomullin, County Clare', *JRSAI,* LXXI, 1941, pp.56-60.
22. H.E. Kilbride-Jones,'Zoomorphic pennanular brooches', *Reports of the Research Committee of the Society of Antiquaries of London*, 1980, p. 1.
23. L. and J. Laing, *op. cit.*, p. 207.
24. H.E. Kilbride-Jones, *op. cit.*, 1980, p.43.
25. B. Cunliffe, 'The Temple of Sulis Minerva at Bath', Volume 2, *The Finds From The Sacred Spring,* Oxford University Committee for Archaeology, Monograph No. 16, 1988, p.23.
26. From a letter to the author of J. Bircher, Keeper of the Collections, Roman Baths Museum, dated 18/2/1999 citing recent research and comments of S. Young.
27. N. Edwards, *The Archaeology of Early Medieval Ireland*, Batsford, London, 1996, p. 133.
28. H.E. Kilbride-Jones, *op. cit.*, p.22; L. and J. Laing, *op. cit*, p. 209.
29. L. and J. Laing, *op. cit.*, p.206.
30. H.E. Kilbride-Jones, *op. cit.*, 1980, p.21.
31. L. and J. Laing, *op. cit.*, p. 203.

CHAPTER 3
1. S. P. Ó Riordáin and J.B. Foy, 'The excavation of Leacanabuaile Stone Fort near Caherciveen, County Kerry', *Journal of the Cork Historical and Archaeological Society*, Part2, Vol. XLVI, No. 164, July-December 1941, p. 85.
2. C.J. Lynn, 'Early Christian Period Domestic Structures: A Change From Round to Rectangular Plans?' *Irish Archaeological Research Forum,* V, 1978, p. 38.
3. F. Mitchell and M. Ryan, *Reading the Irish Landscape,* TownHouse, Dublin, 1998, p. 201.

References

4. D.A Weir, 'Dark Ages and the Pollen Record', *Emania,* No. 11,1993, p.28.
5. S.E. Reeds, 'Agricultural Implements in Prehistoric and Roman Britain', Part I, *BAR* British series 69(I), 1979, pp.60-61.
6. E.C. Cowen, 'Querns', *Antiquity,* 1937, pp. 133-151.
7. S. Culfield, 'The Beehive Quern in Ireland', *JRSAI,* No. 107, 1997, pp.104-138.
8. S. Culfield, *op. cit.,* p.126.
9. B. Raftery, *Pagan Celtic Ireland,* Thames and Hudson, London, 1994, p. 124
10. B. Raftery, *op. cit.,* p. 228.
11. W.E. Boyd, 'Cereal in Scottish Antiquity', *Circea* 5, pp. 101-110.
12. H. Hencken, *op. cit.,* p. 15, p. 242.
13. D.A. Weir, *op. cit.,* p. 26.
14. F. Kelly, 'Early Irish Farming', *Institute for Advanced Studies,* 1997, p.249.
15. Vitruvius, *Architectura,* 10, 4.
16. Plinius, *Historia naturalis* 36,155.
17. Palladius, *De re rustica* I, 42.
18. K.D. White, *Farm Equipment in the Roman World,* Cambridge University Press, 1975, p. 15.
19. F. McCormick, 'Cows, Ringforts and the Origins of Early Christian Ireland', *Emania,* No. 13, 1995, p.35.
20. P. Crabtree, 'Subsistence and Ritual: The Faunal Remains from Dun Ailinne, Co. Kildare', *Emania,* No. 7, 1990, p. 23.
21. D. Ó Cróinín, *Early Medieval Ireland 400-1200,* Longman, 1995, p.99.
22. B. Wailes, Dún Ailinne, 'A Summary Excavation Report', *Emania,* No. 7, 1990, p. 19.
23. F. McCormick, *op. cit.,* No. 13, 1995, p. 35.
24. F. Kelly, *op. cit.,* p. 329.
25. A. Sherratt, 'Plough and pastoralism: aspects of the secondary products rev olution', in H. Hodder, G. Isaac and N. Hammond, *Patterns of the Past: studies in honour of David Clarke,* Cambridge University Press, 1981, p. 284.
26. B.G. Scott, 'The introduction of non-ferrous and ferrous technologies to Ireland: motives and mechanisms', in M. Ryan, *Proceedings V Atlantic Colloqium,* 1979, pp. 189-204.
27. C.J. Lynn, *Some* '"Early" Ring Forts and Crannógs', *The Journal of Irish Archaeology,* I, 1983, p. 56.
28. N. Edwards, *The Archaeology of Early Medieval Ireland,* Batsford,1996,

p. 10.

29. C.J. Lynn, *op. cit.*, p. 56.

30. N. Edwards, *op. cit.*, p. 18.

31. S. Ó Riordáin, 'The excavation of a Large Earthen Ringfort at Garranes, County Cork', *PRIA*, Vol. XLVII, Sect. C, 1942.

32 M.J. Kelly, 'Two Ringforts at Garryduff, County Cork', *PRIA*, Vol. 63, Sect. C, p. 58.

CHAPTER 4

1. R.B. Brash, *The ogham inscribed monuments of the Gaedhil*, 1879, p. 118-119, 217.

2. D. McManus, 'A Guide to Ogam', *An Sagart*, Maynooth County Kildare,1991, p. 60.

3. V.E. Nash-Williams, *The Early Christian Monuments of Wales*, Cardiff, University of Wales Press, 1950, p. 16.

4. A. Weir, *Early Ireland*, Blackstaff Press, Belfast, 1980, p. 155.

5. A. Harvey, 'The Ogham Inscriptions And The Roman Alphabet: Two Traditions or One?', *Archaeology Ireland*, p. 14.

6. A. Ahlqvist, ed., *The Early Irish Linguist*, Helsinki, 1983, pp. 7-10.

7. J. Carney, 'The Invention of the Ogom Cypher', *EIRU,* vol.26, 1975, p. 56.

8. A. Harvey, *op. cit.*, p.14.

9. J. Stevenson, 'The Beginning of Literacy in Ireland', *PRIA*, Vol. 89 C, 1989, p.144, p. 147.

10. D. Rankin, *Celts and the Classical World*, Routledge, London and New York, 1996, p. 26.

11. D. McManus, 'A Chronology of the Latin Loan-Words in Early Irish', *EIRU,* No. 34, 1983, pp 42-43.

12. J. Carney, 'The Old Irish Accentual Poems', *Eiru* XXII,1971, p.69-70.

13. J. Stevenson, 'The Beginning of Literacy in Ireland', *PRIA*, Vol. 89 C, 1989, p. 145.

14. A. Harvey, 'Latin, Literacy and the Celtic Vernaculars Around the Year AD 500', in *Celtic Languages and Celtic Peoples, Proceedings of the Second North American Congress of Celtic Studies* held in Halifax, 16-19 August 1989, edited by C.J. Byrne, M. Harry, P. O'Siadhail, Halifax, Nova Scotia, 1992, p. 22.

15. D. Ó Cróinín, *Early Medieval Ireland*, 400-1200, Longman, London and New York, 1995, p. 169.

REFERENCES

CHAPTER 5

1. D. Flanagan and L. Flanagan, *Irish Place Names*, Gill and Macmillan, Dublin, 1994, p. 35.
2. B. Hodkinson, 'Excavation at Cormac's Chapel, Cashel, 1992 and 1993: A preliminary statement', *Tipperary Historical Journal*, 1994 pp.167-174; and letter from B. Hodkinson to the author dated 14 September 1998.
3. R. Warner, 'The Earliest History of Ireland' in *The Illustrated Archaeology of Ireland*, ed. M. Ryan , 1991, p. 115.
4. B. Raftery, *op. cit.*, p.*219*
5. H. James, *Roman West Wales*, Rampant Press, Camarthen, 1982, p. 30.
6. P.J. Casey, *Roman Coinage in Britain*, Shire Archaeology, Buckinghamshire, 1994, p. 60.
7. D. McManus, *op. cit.*, p. 76, p. 113.
8. A. Way, 'Notice of a stamp used by a Roman oculist or empiric discovered in Ireland', *Archaeological Journal*, 17, 1850, p. 355.
9. R. Jackson, 'A new collyrium-stamp from Staines and some thoughts on eye medicine in Roman London and Britannia, in *Interpreting Roman London, papers in memory of Hug Chapman*, eds. J. Bird, M. Hassall and H. Sheldon, Oxbow monograph 58, Oxford, 1996, p. 180.
10. R.G. Collingwood and R.P. Wright, 'The Roman Inscriptions in Britain, Vol. II, Instrumentum Domesticum, Personal belongings and the like', *RIB* 2446, *Oculists' Stamps*, eds. S.S. Frere and R.S.O. Tomlin, Alan Sutton Publishing, 1992, p. 43.
11. J.P. Mazimann, 'Un nouveau cachet d'oculiste à Mandeure', *Bulletin de la Société d'Emulation de Montbéliard*, No. 117, 1994, p. 109.
12. E. Bourke, 'Stoneyford: a first century Roman burial from Ireland', *Archaeology Ireland*, Vol 3, Number 2, Summer 1989, pp. 56-57.
13. B. Raftery, *op. cit.*, p. 207.
14. P. Salway, *Roman Britain*, Oxford University Press, 1984, p. 378.
15. *Cardiff Castle*, retrieved on 3.8.2000 at: http://www.castlewales.com/cardiff.html
16. M. Dyllon, 'The Irish Settlements in Wales', *Celtica*, Vol. XII, 1977, p. 11.
17. Cormac, Glossary, Y833.
18. C. Thomas, 'The Irish Settlements In Post-Roman Western Britain: A Survey of the Evidence', *Journal of the Royal Institute of Cornwall*, 6 (1969-72), p. 257.
21. H. Mytum, 'Across The Irish Sea: Romano-British and Irish Settlements In Wales', *Emania*, No. 13, 1995, p. 16.

CHAPTER 6

1. P.J. Casey, 'Roman Coinage in Britain', *Sire Archaeology*, Buckinghamshire, 1994, p. 27.
2. From a letter to the author by M.M. Archibald, Department of Coins and Medals, The British Museum, 25 March 1999.
3. R.A.G. Carson and C. O'Kelly, 'A catalogue of the Roman coins from Newgrange, County Meath, and Notes on the coins and Related Finds', *PRIA*, Vol. 77, No. 2, Sect. C, p. 40.
4. Information provided to the author by K. Emerson, Hon. Secretary of the County Donegal Historical Society, letter of 6/2/1997.
5. The Metropolitan Museum of Art, *Treasures of Early Irish Art, 1500 BC to 1500 AD*, New York, 1977, pl. 16.
6. Vita S. Ciarani, Chapter 31.
7. Free translation from: H. von Zimmer, *Über direkte Handelsverbindungen Westgalliens mit Irland im Altertum und frühen Mittelalter,* Sitzungsberichte der Königlich Preussischen Akademie der Wissenschaften, Berlin 1909, p 432
8. Retrieved at http://www.ireland.demon.co.uk/poems.htm#hound of the heroes
9. S.P. Ó Riordáin, 'The Excavation of a large Earthen Ring-Fort at Garranes, County Cork', *PRIA*, Vol XLVII, Sect. C, 1942, p.133
10. M.G. Fulford, 'Byzantium and Britain: a Mediterranean perspective on Post-Roman Mediterranean Imports in western Britain and Ireland', *Medieval Archaeology*, 33 (1989), p. 4
11. D.P. Peacock and D.F. Williams, *Amphorae and the Roman economy: an introductory guide,* Longman, London and New York, 1986, pp.154, 182,186.
12. C. Thomas, 'A Provisional List of Imported pottery in post-Roman Western Britain and Ireland', Institute of Cornish studies, Special report no. 7, 1981, p. 4.
13. H. Mytum, *The Origins of Early Christian Ireland*, Routledge, London and New York, 1992.
14. K. Jermy, *Longford and Langford as Significant Names in Establishing Lines of Roman Roads*, Britannia, Vol. XXIII, 1992, p. 228.
15. Correspondence with the author, 9 February and 28 May 1997.

CHAPTER 7

1. M.J. Green, 'The Gods of Roman Britain', *Shire Archaeology*, Aylesbury,

1983, p. 17.

2. M.J. Green, *The Gods of the Celts*, 1986, Alan Sutton/Barnes and Nobles Books, p. 32.

3. J. Corringwood-Bruce, 'Alnwick Castle', *1880 Catalogue of Antiquities at Alnwick Castle*, Newcastle upon Tyne, p. 93, No. 520.

4. Green, *op. cit.*, 1983, p. 44, p. 59.

5. R.B. Warner, 'Ireland, Ulster and Scotland in the earlier Iron Age', in O'Connor and D.V. Clarke eds., *From the Stone Age to the 'Forty-Five'*, 1983, p. 176 ff.

6. R.A.S. Macalister, *Corpus Inscriptionum Insularum Celticarum*, Vol I, Dublin, Stationery Office, p.302.

7. R.B. Warner, 'The Broighter Hoard: A Reappraisal, And The Iconography of The Collar', in B. Scott ed, *Studies on Early Ireland: Essays in Honour of M.V. Duignan*, 1982, p. 30.

8. R.B. Warner, *op. cit.*, p. 30.

9. R.B. Warner, *op. cit.*, p. 36.

10. C.J. Lynn, 'The Iron age Mound in Navan Fort: A Physical Realisation of Celtic Religious Beliefs?', *Emania*, 1992, pp. 33-57.

11. M.J. Green, *op. cit.*, 1986, p. 45.

12. Diodorus, *Bibliotheca Historica*, II, 47.

13. R. Warner, 'Navan and Apollo', *Emania* 14 (1996) p. 79.

14. R. Warner, *op. cit.*, 14, p. 81.

15. L. de Paor, *The Peoples of Ireland*, Hutchinson, 1986, p. 57

16. H. Mytum, *op. cit.*, p. 15.

17. B. Raftery, *op. cit.*, p. 217.

18. H. Mytum, *op. cit.*, p.40.

19. L. Bieler, 'The Christianisation Of The Insular Celts During The Sub-Roman period and Its Repercussions On The Continent', *Celtica*, Vol. VIII, 1968, p. 114.

20. D. Ó Cróinín, *Early Medieval Ireland*, Longman, London and New York, 1995, p. 22.

21. L. Bieler, *op. cit.*, p. 115.

22. P. Salway, *op. cit.*, p. 464.

23. Ó Cróinín, *op. cit.*, p.190.

24. M. Dillon, 'The Irish settlements In Wales', *Celtica*, Vol. XII, 1977, p. 9

25. H. Mytum, *op. cit.*, p. 38.

26 N. Edwards, *op. cit.*, London, 1990, p. 98.

27. R.A.S. Macalister, *op. cit.*, Vol I, p. 497, No. 519 and Vol. II, p. 114. No. 946, Dublin, Stationery Office, 1949.
28. N. Edwards, *op. cit.*, p. 100.
29. D. Ó Corráin, L. Breatnach, A. Breen, 'The Laws of the Irish', *Peritia*, vol. 3, 1984, p.431
30. H. Mytum, *op. cit.*, p. 46.

CHAPTER 8
1. C. Thomas, 'The Earliest Christian Art in Ireland and Britain', in *Ireland and Insular Art, AD 500-1200, Proceedings of a Conference at University College Cork, 31 October-3 November 1985* edited by M. Ryan, Royal Irish Academy, Dublin, 1987, p. 7.
2. M. Archibald, M. Brown, L. Webster, 'Heirs of Rome: the shaping of Britain, AD 400-900', in *The Transformation of the Roman World, AD 400-900*, L. Webster and M. Brown eds., British Museum Press, 1997, p. 208.
3. L. and J. Laing, *Celtic Britain and Ireland, The Myth of the Dark Ages*, Irish Academic Press, 1990, p. 215.
4. F. Henry, 'Enamels', in *Studies in Early Christian and Medieval Irish art*, Vol. I Enamels and Metalwork, The Pindar Press, London, 1983, p. 5.
5. N. Whitfield, 'Motifs and Techniques of Celtic Filigree: Are They Original?', in *Ireland and Insular Art, AD 500-1200, Proceedings of a Conference at University College Cork, 31 October-3 November 1985* edited by M. Ryan, Royal Irish Academy, Dublin, 1987 p. 83.
6. H. Hencken, *op. cit.*, p. 17.
7. F. Henry, 'Hanging Bowls', *Journal of Royal Society of Antiquaries of Ireland*, No. 66, 1936, pp. 209-246.
8. T. D. Kendrick, British Hanging Bowls, *Antiquity*, No. 6, 1932, pp. 161-184.
9. L. Laing, 'Later Celtic Art in Britain and Ireland', *Shire Archaeology*, 1997, p. 24.
10. F. Henry, 'Hanging Bowls', in *Studies in Early Christian and Medieval Irish Art*, Vol. I, Enamels and Metalwork, The Pindar Press, London, 1983, p. 134
11. R. Bruce-Mitford, 'Ireland and the Hanging-Bowls – A Review', in *Ireland and Insular Art, AD 500-1200, Proceedings of a Conference at University College Cork, 31 October-3 November 1985* edited by M. Ryan, Royal Irish Academy, Dublin, 1987, p. 30.
12. G. Haseloff, 'Insular Animal Styles With Special Reference to Irish Art in the Early Medieval Period', in *Ireland and Insular Art, AD 500-1200, proceed*

REFERENCES

ings of a conference at University College Cork, 31 October-3 November 1985 edited by M. Ryan, Royal Irish Academy, Dublin, 1987, p. 46.

13. M. Ryan, 'The Derrynaflan Hoard and Early Irish Art', in *Speculum,* October 1997, vol. 72, p. 1007.

14. J. Raftery, 'Ex Oriente ...,' *Journal of the Royal Society of Antiquaries of Ireland,* Vol. 95 (1965) p. 196.

15. Raftery, *op. cit.,* p. 203.

16. H. Mattingly and J.W.E. Pearce with a note by T. D. Kendrick, 'The Coleraine Hoard', *Antiquity,* XI, 1937, p. 45.

17. E. Wilson, *8000 Years of Ornament, An Illustrated Handbook of Motifs,* British Museum Press, 1994, p. 181 and p. 191.

INDEX

Aegean pottery, 129
Aesculapius (god of medicine), 136, 143
Aethelred II, king of England, 120
Africa, 51, 118, 129, 162, 164. *see also* Carthage; Egypt; Ethiopia
Agricola, Gnaeus Julius (governor of Britain), 1-2, 4-6, 8-12, 14-17, 21, 25, 30, 34, 108, 110
  death of, 2
  legionary commander, 2, 9, 14
  military career, 1-2, 8-9
  Tacitus' biography, 2, 4, 5-6
agriculture, 61-74
  beans, 66
  beehive querns, 64-66
  cabbage, 66-67
  cereals, 61, 62, 63, 66
  coulter ploughs, 63-64
  dairy farming, 68-70, 72
  enclosed farmsteads, 72
  intensive farming, 62, 68
  new plants, 66-67
  new processes, 67-71
  new techniques, 63-66
  peas, 66
  resurgence of, 61-63
  ringforts, 71-74
  Roman farmsteads, 72
  Roman influences, 61-74
  rotary querns, 64-66
  rye, 66
  vegetables, 66-67
  water mills, 67-68
  wheat, 66
Aibe, Saint, 110
Aix-en-Provence (France), 162
Aix-les-Bains, 148-149
ala, 9
Alaric, king of the Goths, 120
Alauna (Roman fort), 17
Alexandria (Egypt), 116, 121
Alnwick Castle (Northumberland), 138
alpages, 159
Ambracia (Greece), 149
Amiens
  Roman mint, 117
amphorae, trade in, 127-131

Anglesey (Wales), 1, 9
Anglo-Saxon Chronicle, 4
Anglo-Saxons, 4, 46
  art, 165, 173
  graves with hanging bowls, 168-169
  house types, 60
animal representations in Irish art, 164-175, 179
  zoomorphic brooches, 51-54, 56, 165
Annals of the Four Masters, 26, 122
Annaly, princes of, 134
Annan (Roman fort), 17
Antioch, 116
Antiquity, 168
Antrim (County). *see* Armoy; Lyle Hill
Apollo (solar god), 137, 145
  cult of, 145, 147-148
  Greek legend and Irish comparisons, 147-148
Appian way, 132
Aquinum, 7
Arabia, 120
Arcadius (Roman emperor), 115
Archaeological Journal, 99, 100
Archaeology Ireland, 29
archu (hounds), 125
Ardagh chalice, 18, 173
Arezzo, 131
Armagh (city), 144
Armagh (County). *see* Kilnassagart; Navan Fort
Armenia, 20, 174
Armenian war, 13
Armoy (County Antrim), 170
Arretine ware, 131
art. *see* Celtic art; Early Christian art; Irish art; Romano-Celtic art
artefacts. *see also* Irish finds; Roman finds
  provenance problems, 18-19
Artemis, 145
Ashmolean Museum, Oxford, 19, 151
Asia, 162
Asia Minor, 136, 145
Assouan, 162
Athassel Abbey (County Tipperary), 99
Athens (Greece), 129
Attacotti (Irish tribe), 107
Augustus (Roman emperor), 126
Ausonius, 67
Auxonius, 154, 158

193

INDEX